THE PELICAN SHAKESPEARE
GENERAL EDITORS

STEPHEN ORGEL
A. R. BRAUNMULLER

Antony and Cleopatra

Frontispiece to *Antony and Cleopatra*
in Nicholas Rowe's edition of Shakespeare's works, 1709

William Shakespeare

———

Antony and Cleopatra

EDITED BY A. R. BRAUNMULLER

PENGUIN BOOKS

PENGUIN BOOKS
Published by the Penguin Group
Penguin Group (USA) Inc., 375 Hudson Street, New York, New York 10014, U.S.A.
Penguin Books Ltd, 80 Strand, London WC2R 0RL, England
Penguin Books Australia Ltd, 250 Camberwell Road, Camberwell, Victoria 3124, Australia
Penguin Books Canada Ltd, 10 Alcorn Avenue, Toronto, Ontario, Canada M4V 3B2
Penguin Books India (P) Ltd, 11 Community Centre, Panchsheel Park, New Delhi – 110 017, India
Penguin Books (N.Z.) Ltd, Cnr Rosedale and Airborne Roads, Albany, Auckland, New Zealand
Penguin Books (South Africa) (Pty) Ltd, 24 Sturdee Avenue,
Rosebank, Johannesburg 2196, South Africa

Penguin Books Ltd, Registered Offices: 80 Strand, London WC2R 0RL, England

The Tragedy of Antony and Cleopatra edited by Maynard Mack
published in the United States of America
in Penguin Books 1960
Revised edition published 1970
This new edition edited by A. R. Braunmuller published 1999

10

Copyright © Penguin Books Inc., 1960, 1970
Copyright © Penguin Putnam Inc., 1999
All rights reserved

Frontispiece: Courtesy of William Andrews Clark Memorial
Library, University of California, Los Angeles

ISBN 0-14-07.1452-9

Printed in the United States of America
Set in Garamond
Designed by Virginia Norey

Contents

Publisher's Note

IT IS ALMOST half a century since the first volumes of the Pelican Shakespeare appeared under the general editorship of Alfred Harbage. The fact that a new edition, rather than simply a revision, has been undertaken reflects the profound changes textual and critical studies of Shakespeare have undergone in the past twenty years. For the new Pelican series, the texts of the plays and poems have been thoroughly revised in accordance with recent scholarship, and in some cases have been entirely reedited. New introductions and notes have been provided in all the volumes. But the new Shakespeare is also designed as a successor to the original series; the previous editions have been taken into account, and the advice of the previous editors has been solicited where it was feasible to do so.

Certain textual features of the new Pelican Shakespeare should be particularly noted. All lines are numbered that contain a word, phrase, or allusion explained in the glossarial notes. In addition, for convenience, every tenth line is also numbered, in italics when no annotation is indicated. The intrusive and often inaccurate place headings inserted by early editors are omitted (as is becoming standard practice), but for the convenience of those who miss them, an indication of locale now appears as the first item in the annotation of each scene.

In the interest of both elegance and utility, each speech prefix is set in a separate line when the speaker's lines are in verse, except when those words form the second half of a verse line. Thus the verse form of the speech is kept visually intact. What is printed as verse and what is printed as prose has, in general, the authority of the original texts. Departures from the original texts in this regard have only the authority of editorial tradition and the judgment of the Pelican editors; and, in a few instances, are admittedly arbitrary.

The Theatrical World

Economic realities determined the theatrical world in which Shakespeare's plays were written, performed, and received. For centuries in England, the primary theatrical tradition was nonprofessional. Craft guilds (or "mysteries") provided religious drama – mystery plays – as part of the celebration of religious and civic festivals, and schools and universities staged classical and neoclassical drama in both Latin and English as part of their curricula. In these forms, drama was established and socially acceptable. Professional theater, in contrast, existed on the margins of society. The acting companies were itinerant; playhouses could be any available space – the great halls of the aristocracy, town squares, civic halls, inn yards, fair booths, or open fields – and income was sporadic, dependent on the passing of the hat or on the bounty of local patrons. The actors, moreover, were considered little better than vagabonds, constantly in danger of arrest or expulsion.

In the late 1560s and 1570s, however, English professional theater began to gain respectability. Wealthy aristocrats fond of drama – the Lord Admiral, for example, or the Lord Chamberlain – took acting companies under their protection so that the players technically became members of their households and were no longer subject to arrest as homeless or masterless men. Permanent theaters were first built at this time as well, allowing the companies to control and charge for entry to their performances.

Shakespeare's livelihood, and the stunning artistic explosion in which he participated, depended on pragmatic and architectural effort. Professional theater requires ways to restrict access to its offerings; if it does not, and admission fees cannot be charged, the actors do not get paid, the costumes go to a pawnbroker, and there is no such thing as a professional, ongoing theatrical tradition. The answer to that economic need arrived in the late 1560s and 1570s with the creation of the so-called public or amphitheater playhouse. Recent discoveries indicate that the precursor of the Globe playhouse in London (where Shakespeare's mature plays were presented) and the Rose theater (which presented Christopher Marlowe's plays and some of Shakespeare's earliest ones) was the Red Lion theater of 1567. Archaeological studies of the foundations of the Rose and Globe theaters have revealed that the open-air theater of the 1590s and later was probably a polygonal building with fourteen to twenty or twenty-four sides, multistoried, from 75 to 100 feet in diameter, with a raised, partly covered "thrust" stage that projected into a group of standing patrons, or "groundlings," and a covered gallery, seating up to 2,500 or more (very crowded) spectators.

These theaters might have been about half full on any given day, though the audiences were larger on holidays or when a play was advertised, as old and new were, through printed playbills posted around London. The metropolitan area's late-Tudor, early-Stuart population (circa 1590-1620) has been estimated at about 150,000 to 250,000. It has been supposed that in the mid-1590s there were about 15,000 spectators per week at the public theaters; thus, as many as 10 percent of the local population went to the theater regularly. Consequently, the theaters' repertories – the plays available for this experienced and frequent audience – had to change often: in the month between September 15 and October 15, 1595, for instance, the Lord Admiral's Men performed twenty-eight times in eighteen different plays.

Since natural light illuminated the amphitheaters' stages, performances began between noon and two o'clock and ran without a break for two or three hours. They often concluded with a jig, a fencing display, or some other nondramatic exhibition. Weather conditions deter-

mined the season for the amphitheaters: plays were performed every day (including Sundays, sometimes, to cler-
ical dismay) except during Lent – the forty days before
Easter – or periods of plague, or sometimes during the
summer months when law courts were not in session and
the most affluent members of the audience were not in
London.

To a modern theatergoer, an amphitheater stage like
that of the Rose or Globe would appear an unfamiliar mix-
ture of plainness and elaborate decoration. Much of the
structure was carved or painted, sometimes to imitate
marble; elsewhere, as under the canopy projecting over the
stage, to represent the stars and the zodiac. Appropriate
painted canvas pictures (of Jerusalem, for example, if the
play was set in that city) were apparently hung on the wall
behind the acting area, and tragedies were accompanied by
black hangings, presumably something like crepe festoons
or bunting. Although these theaters did not employ what
we would call scenery, early modern spectators saw numerous large props, such as the "bar" at which a prisoner stood
during a trial, the "mossy bank" where lovers reclined,
an arbor for amorous conversation, a chariot, gallows,
tables, trees, beds, thrones, writing desks, and so forth.
Audiences might learn a scene's location from a sign (reading "Athens," for example) carried across the stage (as in
Bertolt Brecht's twentieth-century productions). Equally
captivating (and equally irritating to the theater's enemies)
were the rich costumes and personal props the actors used:
the most valuable items in the surviving theatrical invento-
ries are the swords, gowns, robes, crowns, and other items
worn or carried by the performers.

Magic appealed to Shakespeare's audiences as much as
it does to us today, and the theater exploited many decep-
tive and spectacular devices. A winch in the loft above the
stage, called "the heavens," could lower and raise actors
playing gods, goddesses, and other supernatural figures to
and from the main acting area, just as one or more trap-
doors permitted entrances and exits to and from the area,

called "hell," beneath the stage. Actors wore elementary makeup such as wigs, false beards, and face paint, and they employed pig's bladders filled with animal blood to make wounds seem more real. They had rudimentary but effective ways of pretending to behead or hang a person. Supernumeraries (stagehands or actors not needed in a particular scene) could make thunder sounds (by shaking a metal sheet or rolling an iron ball down a chute) and show lightning (by blowing inflammable resin through tubes into a flame). Elaborate fireworks enhanced the effects of dragons flying through the air or imitated such celestial phenomena as comets, shooting stars, and multiple suns. Horses' hoofbeats, bells (located perhaps in the tower above the stage), trumpets and drums, clocks, cannon shots and gunshots, and the like were common sound effects. And the music of viols, cornets, oboes, and recorders was a regular feature of theatrical performances.

For two relatively brief spans, from the late 1570s to 1590 and from 1599 to 1614, the amphitheaters competed with the so-called private, or indoor, theaters, which originated as, or later represented themselves as, educational institutions training boys as singers for church services and court performances. These indoor theaters had two features that were distinct from the amphitheaters': their personnel and their playing spaces. The amphitheaters' adult companies included both adult men, who played the male roles, and boys, who played the female roles; the private, or indoor, theater companies, on the other hand, were entirely composed of boys aged about 8 to 16, who were, or could pretend to be, candidates for singers in a church or a royal boys' choir. (Until 1660, professional theatrical companies included no women.) The playing space would appear much more familiar to modern audiences than the long-vanished amphitheaters; the later indoor theaters were, in fact, the ancestors of the typical modern theater. They were enclosed spaces, usually rectangular, with the stage filling one end of the rectangle and the audience arrayed in seats or benches across (and sometimes lining) the building's longer axis. These spaces staged plays less frequently than the public theaters (perhaps only once a week) and held far fewer spectators than the amphitheaters: about 200 to 600, as opposed to 2,500 or more. Fewer patrons mean a smaller gross income, unless each pays more. Not surprisingly, then, private theaters charged higher prices than the amphitheaters, probably sixpence, as opposed to a penny for the cheapest entry.

Protected from the weather, the indoor theaters presented plays later in the day than the amphitheaters, and used artificial illumination – candles in sconces or candelabra. But candles melt, and need replacing, snuffing, and trimming, and these practical requirements may have been part of the reason the indoor theaters introduced breaks in the performance, the intermission so dear to the heart of theatergoers and to the pocketbooks of theater concessionaires ever since. Whether motivated by the need to tend to the candles or by the entrepreneurs' wishing to sell oranges and liquor, or both, the indoor theaters eventually established the modern convention of the non-continuous performance. In the early modern "private" theater, musical performances apparently filled the intermissions, which in Stuart theater jargon seem to have been called "acts."

At the end of the first decade of the seventeenth century, the distinction between public amphitheaters and private indoor companies ceased. For various cultural, political, and economic reasons, individual companies gained control of both the public, open-air theaters and the indoor ones, and companies mixing adult men and boys took over the formerly "private" theaters. Despite the death of the boys' companies and of their highly innovative theaters (for which such luminous playwrights as Ben Jonson, George Chapman, and John Marston wrote), their playing spaces and conventions had an immense impact on subsequent plays: not merely for the intervals (which stressed the artistic and architectonic importance of "acts"), but also because they introduced political and social satire as a popular dramatic ingredient, even in tragedy, and a wider range of actorly effects, encouraged by their more intimate playing spaces.

Even the briefest sketch of the Shakespearean theatrical world would be incomplete without some comment on the social and cultural dimensions of theaters and playing in the period. In an intensely hierarchical and status-conscious society, professional actors and their ventures had hardly any respectability; as we have indicated, to protect themselves against laws designed to curb vagabondage and the increase of masterless men, actors resorted to the near-fiction that they were the servants of noble masters, and wore their distinctive livery. Hence the company for which Shakespeare wrote in the 1590s called itself the Lord Chamberlain's Men and pretended that the public, money-getting performances were in fact rehearsals for private per-formances before that high court official. From 1598, the Privy Council had licensed theatrical companies, and after 1603, with the accession of King James I, the companies gained explicit royal protection, just as the Queen's Men had for a time under Queen Elizabeth. The Chamberlain's Men became the King's Men, and the other companies were patronized by the other members of the royal family.

These designations were legal fictions that half-concealed an important economic and social develop-ment, the evolution away from the theater's organization on the model of the guild, a self-regulating confraternity of individual artisans, into a proto-capitalist organization. Shakespeare's company became a joint-stock company, where persons who supplied capital and, in some cases, such as Shakespeare's, capital and talent, employed them-selves and others in earning a return on that capital. This development meant that actors and theater companies were outside both the traditional guild structures, which required some form of civic or royal charter, and the feu-dal household organization of master-and-servant. This anomalous, maverick social and economic condition

made theater companies practically unruly and poten-
tially even dangerous; consequently, numerous official
bodies – including the London metropolitan and ecclesi-
astical authorities as well as, occasionally, the royal court
itself – tried, without much success, to control and even
to disband them.

Public officials had good reason to want to close the
theaters: they were attractive nuisances – they drew often
riotous crowds, they were always noisy, and they could be
politically offensive and socially insubordinate. Until the
Civil War, however, anti-theatrical forces failed to shut
down professional theater, for many reasons – limited
surveillance and few police powers, tensions or outright
hostilities among the agencies that sought to check or
channel theatrical activity, and lack of clear policies for
control. Another reason must have been the theaters' un-
deniable popularity. Curtailing any activity enjoyed by
such a substantial percentage of the population was difficult, as various Roman emperors attempting to limit cir-
cuses had learned, and the Tudor-Stuart audience was not
merely large, it was socially diverse and included women.
The prevalence of public entertainment in this period
has been underestimated. In fact, fairs, holidays, games,
sporting events, the equivalent of modern parades, freak
shows, and street exhibitions all abounded, but the theater was the most widely and frequently available entertainment to which people of every class had access. That
fact helps account both for its quantity and for the fear
and anger it aroused.

WILLIAM SHAKESPEARE OF
STRATFORD-UPON-AVON, GENTLEMAN

Many people have said that we know very little about
William Shakespeare's life – pinheads and postcards are
often mentioned as appropriately tiny surfaces on which
to record the available information. More imaginatively

and perhaps more correctly, Ralph Waldo Emerson wrote, "Shakespeare is the only biographer of Shakespeare. . . . So far from Shakespeare's being the least known, he is the one person in all modern history fully known to us."

In fact, we know more about Shakespeare's life than we do about almost any other English writer's of his era. His last will and testament (dated March 25, 1616) survives, as do numerous legal contracts and court documents involving Shakespeare as principal or witness, and parish records in Stratford and London. Shakespeare appears quite often in official records of King James's royal court, and of course Shakespeare's name appears on numerous title pages and in the written and recorded words of his literary contemporaries Robert Greene, Henry Chettle, Francis Meres, John Davies of Hereford, Ben Jonson, and many others. Indeed, if we make due allowance for the bloating of modern, run-of-the-mill bureaucratic records, more information has survived over the past four hundred years about William Shakespeare of Stratford-upon-Avon, Warwickshire, than is likely to survive in the next four hundred years about any reader of these words.

What we do not have are entire categories of information – Shakespeare's private letters or diaries, drafts and revisions of poems and plays, critical prefaces or essays, commendatory verse for other writers' works, or instructions guiding his fellow actors in their performances, for instance – that we imagine would help us understand and appreciate his surviving writings. For all we know, many such data never existed as written records. Many literary and theatrical critics, not knowing what might once have existed, more or less cheerfully accept the situation; some even make a theoretical virtue of it by claiming that such data are irrelevant to understanding and interpreting the plays and poems.

So, what do we know about William Shakespeare, the man responsible for thirty-seven or perhaps more plays, more than 150 sonnets, two lengthy narrative poems, and some shorter poems?

While many families by the name of Shakespeare (or some variant spelling) can be identified in the English Midlands as far back as the twelfth century, it seems likely that the dramatist's grandfather, Richard, moved to Snitterfield, a town not far from Stratford-upon-Avon, sometime before 1529. In Snitterfield, Richard Shakespeare leased farmland from the very wealthy Robert Arden. By 1552, Richard's son John had moved to a large house on Henley Street in Stratford-upon-Avon, the house that stands today as "The Birthplace." In Stratford, John Shakespeare traded as a glover, dealt in wool, and lent money at interest; he also served in a variety of civic posts, including "High Bailiff," the municipality's equivalent of mayor. In 1557, he married Robert Arden's youngest daughter, Mary. Mary and John had four sons – William was the oldest – and four daughters, of whom only Joan outlived her most celebrated sibling. William was baptized (an event entered in the Stratford parish church records) on April 26, 1564, and it has become customary, without any good factual support, to suppose he was born on April 23, which happens to be the feast day of Saint George, patron saint of England, and is also the date on which he died, in 1616. Shakespeare married Anne Hathaway in 1582, when he was eighteen and she was twenty-six; their first child was born five months later. It has been generally assumed that the marriage was enforced and subsequently unhappy, but these are only assumptions; it has been estimated, for instance, that up to one third of Elizabethan brides were pregnant when they married. Anne and William Shakespeare had three children: Susanna, who married a prominent local physician, John Hall; and the twins Hamnet, who died young in 1596, and Judith, who married Thomas Quiney – apparently a rather shady individual. The name Hamnet was unusual but not unique: he and his twin sister were named for their godparents, Shakespeare's neighbors Hamnet and Judith Sadler. Shakespeare's father died in 1601 (the year of *Hamlet*), and Mary Arden Shakespeare died in 1608 (the year of *Coriolanus*). William Shakespeare's last surviving direct descendant was his granddaughter Elizabeth Hall, who died in 1670.

Between the birth of the twins in 1585 and a clear reference to Shakespeare as a practicing London dramatist in Robert Greene's sensationalizing, satiric pamphlet, *Greene's Groatsworth of Wit* (1592), there is no record of where William Shakespeare was or what he was doing. These seven so-called lost years have been imaginatively filled by scholars and other students of Shakespeare: some think he traveled to Italy, or fought in the Low Countries, or studied law or medicine, or worked as an apprentice actor/writer, and so on to even more fanciful possibilities. Whatever the biographical facts for those "lost" years, Greene's nasty remarks in 1592 testify to professional envy and to the fact that Shakespeare already had a successful career in London. Speaking to his fellow playwrights, Greene warns both generally and specifically:

> ... trust them [actors] not: for there is an upstart crow, beautified with our feathers, that with his tiger's heart wrapped in a player's hide supposes he is as well able to bombast out a blank verse as the best of you; and being an absolute Johannes Factotum, is in his own conceit the only Shake-scene in a country.

The passage mimics a line from *3 Henry VI* (hence the play must have been performed before Greene wrote) and seems to say that "Shake-scene" is both actor and playwright, a jack-of-all-trades. That same year, Henry Chettle protested Greene's remarks in *Kind-Heart's Dream,* and each of the next two years saw the publication of poems – *Venus and Adonis* and *The Rape of Lucrece,* respectively – publicly ascribed to (and dedicated by) Shakespeare. Early in 1595 he was named one of the senior members of a prominent acting company, the Lord Chamberlain's Men, when they received payment for court performances during the 1594 Christmas season.

Clearly, Shakespeare had achieved both success and reputation in London. In 1596, upon Shakespeare's application, the College of Arms granted his father the now-familiar coat of arms he had taken the first steps to obtain almost twenty years before, and in 1598, John's son – now permitted to call himself "gentleman" – took a 10 percent share in the new Globe playhouse. In 1597, he bought a substantial bourgeois house, called New Place, in Stratford – the garden remains, but Shakespeare's house, several times rebuilt, was torn down in 1759 – and over the next few years Shakespeare spent large sums buying land and making other investments in the town and its environs. Though he worked in London, his family remained in Stratford, and he seems always to have considered Stratford the home he would eventually return to. Something approaching a disinterested appreciation of Shakespeare's popular and professional status appears in Francis Meres's *Palladis Tamia* (1598), a not especially imaginative and perhaps therefore persuasive record of literary reputations. Reviewing contemporary English writers, Meres lists the titles of many of Shakespeare's plays, including one not now known, *Love's Labor's Won,* and praises his "mellifluous & hony-tongued" "sugred Sonnets," which were then circulating in manuscript (they were first collected in 1609). Meres describes Shakespeare as "one of the best" English playwrights of both comedy and tragedy. In *Remains . . . Concerning Britain* (1605), William Camden – a more authoritative source than the imitative Meres – calls Shakespeare one of the "most pregnant witts of these our times" and joins him with such writers as Chapman, Daniel, Jonson, Marston, and Spenser. During the first decades of the seventeenth century, publishers began to attribute numerous play quartos, including some non-Shakespearean ones, to Shakespeare, either by name or initials, and we may assume that they deemed Shakespeare's name and supposed authorship, true or false, commercially attractive.

For the next ten years or so, various records show

Shakespeare's dual career as playwright and man of the theater in London, and as an important local figure in Stratford. In 1608-9 his acting company – designated the "King's Men" soon after King James had succeeded Queen Elizabeth in 1603 – rented, refurbished, and opened a small interior playing space, the Blackfriars theater, in London, and Shakespeare was once again listed as a substantial sharer in the group of proprietors of the playhouse. By May 11, 1612, however, he describes himself as a Stratford resident in a London lawsuit – an indication that he had withdrawn from day-to-day professional activity and returned to the town where he had always had his main financial interests. When Shakespeare bought a substantial residential building in London, the Blackfriars Gatehouse, close to the theater of the same name, on March 10, 1613, he is recorded as William Shakespeare "of Stratford upon Avon in the county of Warwick, gentleman," and he named several London residents as the building's trustees. Still, he continued to participate in theatrical activity: when the new Earl of Rutland needed an allegorical design to bear as a shield, or *impresa,* at the celebration of King James's Accession Day, March 24, 1613, the earl's accountant recorded a payment of 44 shillings to Shakespeare for the device with its motto.

For the last few years of his life, Shakespeare evidently concentrated his activities in the town of his birth. Most of the final records concern business transactions in Stratford, ending with the notation of his death on April 23, 1616, and burial in Holy Trinity Church, Stratford-upon-Avon.

The Question of Authorship

The history of ascribing Shakespeare's plays (the poems do not come up so often) to someone else began, as it continues, peculiarly. The earliest published claim that someone else wrote Shakespeare's plays appeared in an 1856 article by Delia Bacon in the American journal *Putnam's Monthly* – although an Englishman, Thomas Wilmot, had shared his doubts in private (even secretive) conversations with friends near the end of the eighteenth century. Bacon's was a sad personal history that ended in madness and poverty, but the year after her article, she published, with great difficulty and the bemused assistance of Nathaniel Hawthorne (then United States Consul in Liverpool, England), her *Philosophy of the Plays of Shakspere Unfolded*. This huge, ornately written, confusing farrago is almost unreadable; sometimes its intents, to say nothing of its arguments, disappear entirely beneath near-raving, ecstatic writing. Tumbled in with much supposed "philosophy" appear the claims that Francis Bacon (from whom Delia Bacon eventually claimed descent), Walter Ralegh, and several other contemporaries of Shakespeare's had written the plays. The book had little impact except as a ridiculed curiosity.

Once proposed, however, the issue gained momentum among people whose conviction was the greater in proportion to their ignorance of sixteenth- and seventeenth-century English literature, history, and society. Another American amateur, Catherine P. Ashmead Windle, made the next influential contribution to the cause when she published *Report to the British Museum* (1882), wherein she promised to open "the Cipher of Francis Bacon," though what she mostly offers, in the words of S. Schoenbaum, is "demented allegorizing." An entire new cottage industry grew from Windle's suggestion that the texts contain hidden, cryptographically discoverable ciphers – "clues" – to their authorship; and today there are not only books devoted to the putative ciphers, but also pamphlets, journals, and newsletters.

Although Baconians have led the pack of those seeking a substitute Shakespeare, in *"Shakespeare" Identified* (1920), J. Thomas Looney became the first published

"Oxfordian" when he proposed Edward de Vere, seventeenth earl of Oxford, as the secret author of Shakespeare's plays. Also for Oxford and his "authorship" there are today dedicated societies, articles, journals, and books. Less popular candidates – Queen Elizabeth and Christopher Marlowe among them – have had adherents, but the movement seems to have divided into two main contending factions, Baconian and Oxfordian. (For further details on all the candidates for "Shakespeare," see S. Schoenbaum, *Shakespeare's Lives*, 2nd ed., 1991.)

The Baconians, the Oxfordians, and supporters of other candidates have one trait in common – they are snobs. Every pro-Bacon or pro-Oxford tract sooner or later claims that the historical William Shakespeare of Stratford-upon-Avon could not have written the plays because he could not have had the training, the university education, the experience, and indeed the imagination or background their author supposedly possessed. Only a learned genius like Bacon or an aristocrat like Oxford could have written such fine plays. (As it happens, lucky male children of the middle class had access to better education than most aristocrats in Elizabethan England – and Oxford was not particularly well educated.) Shakespeare received in the Stratford grammar school a formal education that would daunt many college graduates today; and popular rival playwrights such as the very learned Ben Jonson and George Chapman, both of whom also lacked university training, achieved great artistic success, without being taken as Bacon or Oxford.

Besides snobbery, one other quality characterizes the authorship controversy: lack of evidence. A great deal of testimony from Shakespeare's time shows that Shakespeare wrote Shakespeare's plays and that his contemporaries recognized them as distinctive and distinctly superior. (Some of that contemporary evidence is collected in E. K. Chambers, *William Shakespeare: A Study of Facts and Problems*, 2 vols., 1930.) Since that testimony comes from Shakespeare's enemies and theatrical competitors as well as from his co-workers and from the Elizabethan equivalent of literary journalists, it seems unlikely that, if any one of these sources had known he was a fraud, they would have failed to record that fact.

Books About Shakespeare's Theater

Useful scholarly studies of theatrical life in Shakespeare's day include: G. E. Bentley, *The Jacobean and Caroline Stage,* 7 vols. (1941-68), and the same author's *The Professions of Dramatist and Player in Shakespeare's Time, 1590-1642* (1986); E. K. Chambers, *The Elizabethan Stage,* 4 vols. (1923); R. A. Foakes, *Illustrations of the English Stage, 1580-1642* (1985); Andrew Gurr, *The Shakespearean Stage,* 3rd ed. (1992), and the same author's *Play-going in Shakespeare's London,* 2nd ed. (1996); Edwin Nungezer, *A Dictionary of Actors* (1929); Carol Chillington Rutter, ed., *Documents of the Rose Playhouse* (1984).

Books About Shakespeare's Life

The following books provide scholarly, documented accounts of Shakespeare's life: G. E. Bentley, *Shakespeare: A Biographical Handbook* (1961); E. K. Chambers, *William Shakespeare: A Study of Facts and Problems,* 2 vols. (1930); S. Schoenbaum, *William Shakespeare: A Compact Documentary Life* (1977); and *Shakespeare's Lives,* 2nd ed. (1991), by the same author. Many scholarly editions of Shakespeare's complete works print brief compilations of essential dates and events. References to Shakespeare's works up to 1700 are collected in C. M. Ingleby et al., *The Shakespeare Allusion-Book,* rev. ed., 2 vols. (1932).

The Texts of Shakespeare

As FAR AS WE KNOW, only one manuscript conceivably in Shakespeare's own hand may (and even this is much disputed) exist: a few pages of a play called *Sir Thomas More,* which apparently was never performed. What we do have, as later readers, performers, scholars, students, are printed texts. The earliest of these survive in two forms: quartos and folios. Quartos (from the Latin for "four") are small books, printed on sheets of paper that were then folded in fours, to make eight double-sided pages. When these were bound together, the result was a squarish, eminently portable volume that sold for the relatively small sum of sixpence (translating in modern terms to about $5.00). In folios, on the other hand, the sheets are folded only once, in half, producing large, impressive volumes taller than they are wide. This was the format for important works of philosophy, science, theology, and literature (the major precedent for a folio Shakespeare was Ben Jonson's *Works,* 1616). The decision to print the works of a popular playwright in folio is an indication of how far up on the social scale the theatrical profession had come during Shakespeare's lifetime. The Shakespeare folio was an expensive book, selling for between fifteen and eighteen shillings, depending on the binding (in modern terms, from about $150 to $180). Twenty Shakespeare plays of the thirty-seven that survive first appeared in quarto, seventeen of which appeared during Shakespeare's lifetime; the rest of the plays are found only in folio.

The First Folio was published in 1623, seven years after Shakespeare's death, and was authorized by his fellow actors, the co-owners of the King's Men. This publication was certainly a mark of the company's enormous respect for Shakespeare; but it was also a way of turning the old plays, most of which were no longer current in the play-house, into ready money (the folio includes only Shake-speare's plays, not his sonnets or other nondramatic verse). Whatever the motives behind the publication of the folio, the texts it preserves constitute the basis for almost all later editions of the playwright's works. The texts, however, dif-fer from those of the earlier quartos, sometimes in minor respects but often significantly – most strikingly in the two texts of *King Lear,* but also in important ways in *Hamlet, Othello,* and *Troilus and Cressida.* (The variants are recorded in the textual notes to each play in the new Pelican series.) The differences in these texts represent, in a sense, the essence of theater: the texts of plays were ini-tially not intended for publication. They were scripts, de-signed for the actors to perform – the principal life of the play at this period was in performance. And it follows that in Shakespeare's theater the playwright typically had no say either in how his play was performed or in the disposi-tion of his text – he was an employee of the company. The authoritative figures in the theatrical enterprise were the shareholders in the company, who were for the most part the major actors. They decided what plays were to be done; they hired the playwright and often gave him an outline of the play they wanted him to write. Often, too, the play was a collaboration: the company would retain a group of writers, and parcel out the scenes among them. The resulting script was then the property of the com-pany, and the actors would revise it as they saw fit during the course of putting it on stage. The resulting text be-longed to the company. The playwright had no rights in it once he had been paid. (This system survives largely intact in the movie industry, and most of the playwrights of Shakespeare's time were as anonymous as most screenwrit-ers are today.) The script could also, of course, continue to change as the tastes of audiences and the requirements of the actors changed. Many – perhaps most – plays were re-vised when they were reintroduced after any substantial absence from the repertory, or when they were performed by a company different from the one that originally commissioned the play.

Shakespeare was an exceptional figure in this world because he was not only a shareholder and actor in his company, but also its leading playwright – he was literally his own boss. He had, moreover, little interest in the publication of his plays, and even those that appeared during his lifetime with the authorization of the company show no signs of any editorial concern on the part of the author. Theater was, for Shakespeare, a fluid and supremely responsive medium – the very opposite of the great classic canonical text that has embodied his works since 1623.

The very fluidity of the original texts, however, has meant that Shakespeare has always had to be edited. Here is an example of how problematic the editorial project inevitably is, a passage from the most famous speech in *Romeo and Juliet,* Juliet's balcony soliloquy beginning "O Romeo, Romeo, wherefore art thou Romeo?" Since the eighteenth century, the standard modern text has read,

> What's Montague? It is nor hand, nor foot,
> Nor arm, nor face, nor any other part
> Belonging to a man. O be some other name!
> What's in a name? That which we call a rose
> By any other name would smell as sweet.
> (II.2.40-44)

Editors have three early texts of this play to work from, two quarto texts and the folio. Here is how the First Quarto (1597) reads:

> Whats *Mountague?* It is nor hand nor foote,
> Nor arme, nor face, nor any other part.
> Whats in a name? That which we call a Rose,
> By any other name would smell as sweet:

Here is the Second Quarto (1599):

> Whats *Mountague*? it is nor hand nor foote,
> Nor arme nor face, ô be some other name
> Belonging to a man.
> Whats in a name that which we call a rose,
> By any other word would smell as sweete,

And here is the First Folio (1623):

> What's *Mountague*? it is nor hand nor foote,
> Nor arme, nor face, O be some other name
> Belonging to a man.
> What? in a names that which we call a Rose,
> By any other word would smell as sweete,

There is in fact no early text that reads as our modern text does – and this is the most famous speech in the play. Instead, we have three quite different texts, all of which are clearly some version of the same speech, but none of which seems to us a final or satisfactory version. The transcendently beautiful passage in modern editions is an editorial invention: editors have succeeded in conflating and revising the three versions into something we recognize as great poetry. Is this what Shakespeare "really" wrote? Who can say? What we can say is that Shakespeare always had performance, not a book, in mind.

Books About the Shakespeare Texts

The standard study of the printing history of the First Folio is W. W. Greg, *The Shakespeare First Folio* (1955). J. K. Walton, *The Quarto Copy for the First Folio of Shakespeare* (1971), is a useful survey of the relation of the quartos to the folio. The second edition of Charlton Hinman's *Norton Facsimile* of the First Folio (1996), with a new introduction by Peter Blayney, is indispensable. Stanley Wells and Gary Taylor, *William Shakespeare: A Textual Companion*, keyed to the Oxford text, gives a comprehensive survey of the editorial situation for all the plays and poems.

THE GENERAL EDITORS

Introduction

An enduring medieval myth held that refugees from the Trojan War founded Britain. Trojan survivors, led by King Priam's son Aeneas, traveled first to Africa (where their leader wooed and abandoned the Carthaginian queen, Dido, an episode recalled in *Antony and Cleopatra*); thence to Italy, where they founded the Roman imperium; and then farther, under the leadership of Brut/Brit to *Brit*ain, where they built New Troy (London) and gave Shakespeare's first audiences a "foundation myth." Although sixteenth- and seventeenth-century historians challenged this myth, Shakespeare's audiences could and did see themselves as inheriting classical values and, along with those values, ancient enmities and prejudices. They could, thus, see themselves as inheritors of the Roman republic and, more frequently, the Roman empire. They could also see themselves as successors to Troy's culture (as opposed to that of Greece), and they could see themselves as having an intellectual, historical, even political, stake in the greatest preclassical civilization they knew, Ptolemaic Egypt, which was historically a Greek dominion.

King James I, who ascended the English throne in 1603, immediately became the official patron of Shakespeare's theater company. When Shakespeare and the first audiences of *Antony and Cleopatra* looked to their new king, they might well have seen confirmed a symbolic link with classical Rome. King James, his publicists, and his client-artists often represented the English king as "Caesar," his reign as classically imperial, and his diplomatic and commercial policies as a renewal of Rome's history. As English explorers and then colonists more and more traveled into North America, it is not far-fetched to suppose that Shakespeare's audiences conceived their nation as replicating in the "New World" the imperial domination of Rome in the Old.

In Cecil B. DeMille's 1934 movie *Cleopatra,* a character at a Roman dinner party asks, "Is Cleopatra black?" She is laughed down scornfully, yet the racial question is also a question about colonialism and the conquest of one people by another. As Shakespeare's main source, Plutarch's lengthy parallels between Greek and Roman notables, and one of Shakespeare's minor sources, Samuel Daniel's play *Cleopatra* (first published in 1594, revised and republished in 1599, still further revised – apparently in response to Shakespeare's play – and republished in 1607), make quite clear, the historical Cleopatra was of Macedonian-Greek descent, a member of the class and nationality that had ruled Egypt since Alexander the Great's conquest (332 B.C.) for three centuries before the historical period (approximately 40-30 B.C.) of Shakespeare's play. Shakespeare's, and his audience's, knowledge of and attitudes toward race, ethnicity, and related subjects are, however, extremely hard to define, even in our deeply confused modern terminology. For Shakespeare and us, the question extends from Shylock (a Jew) and the Moorish Prince of Morocco in *The Merchant of Venice* to Aaron in *Titus Andronicus* to Othello (both also Moors) to Caliban in *The Tempest.*

Roman speakers ladle Elizabethan-specific opprobrium – "witch," "fairy," "enchantress" – on Cleopatra, and the terms mark her as a stranger, dangerous and extra-humanly powerful, a being who threatens not just the play's imagined "Roman" order and reason but who could evoke some deeply felt English fears, or at least worries. It is unlikely that those fears were specifically racial rather than nationalistic or religious, that the earliest and later audiences understood Cleopatra as "black" rather than "Eastern" or "Asiatic," themselves strong markers of difference. The angriest, most unsophisticated, and possibly racist hostility toward Cleopatra occurs at the play's very

start and therefore may establish attitudes to be confirmed or denied later. Evidently a loyal but disgusted
Roman soldier, the play's first speaker, one Philo, claims
that Antony's "goodly eyes"

> . . . now bend, now turn
> The office and devotion of their view
> Upon a tawny front. . . .

Philo concludes that Antony's "captain's heart . . . reneges
all temper / And is become the bellows and the fan / To
cool a gypsy's lust."

Romany people, dark-haired, dark-skinned, and ulti-
mately of northern Indian origin, had begun to enter England in the sixteenth century, where they were named, as
in other European languages, with a derivative of "Egyptian" – Gypsies. To call Egyptian Cleopatra a "gypsy"
comes easily to Philo's lips and is satisfyingly insulting –
just as it is when Antony describes her as "like a right
gypsy" (IV.12.28) when he thinks she has sold out to Caesar. The epithet insults Cleopatra, though, only if she is
not and was not generally considered to be a dark-skinned
Romany and therefore, from a racist point of view, ugly or
otherwise repellent or threatening. Since the historical
Cleopatra was Greek-descended, all this makes good color
sense and good vituperation. Most knowledgeable Eliza-
bethans would probably have agreed with Mercutio, who
thinks Cleopatra was no more a "gypsy" than Petrarch's
Laura was a washer wench (*Romeo and Juliet,* II.4).

Philo's other obvious insult is "tawny." Like most color
words, "tawny" is hard to define historically; it seems to
have meant some brownish color, and Shakespeare elsewhere uses it to describe suntanned or sunburnt skin,
which Elizabethan canons of beauty regarded as undesir-
able. "Front" does punful double duty: it means "forehead" and "military front lines" – Antony advances his
arms against a dark-skinned foe. Almost as early in the
play, Cleopatra describes herself as "with Phoebus' amorous

pinches black"(I.5.28). The plain interpretation of her re-
mark is that she has tan skin, pinched and therefore
bruised (black-and-blue), by the sun god, Phoebus.

Performances shape this speech variously. Cleopatra
here recollects her earlier relations with Antony while he
is away in Rome: she may be exaggerating her undesir-
able, wrinkled, aged appearance; she may be remarking
how wonderful Antony found her despite that appearance; she may be noting how beautiful she is, however her
Roman enemies might try to make her appear unattrac-
tive. Cleopatra's motives are, as usual, opaque. As the play
represents the racial issues, none of the possible choices
available to an early modern English audience stresses her
racial "blackness" as a component of her exotic beauty or
ugliness.

For Shakespeare's Christian audience, the play's references to "Herod of Jewry" and "Great Herod" (I.2.29-30;
III.3.3; III.6.73; IV.6.14) injected another set of cultural
perceptions of difference, including the divisive issue of
Jesus' execution. Historically, Herod was indeed "Great
Herod," Herod the Great (73-4 B.C.), a violent man
whom Antony and the play's Caesar sponsored as Judea's
ruler, and a king toward whom Cleopatra was unrelent-
ingly hostile in support of her own territorial ambitions –
"That Herod's head / I'll have" (III.3.4-5). This Herod's
two sons, Herod Archelaus and Herod Antipas, both later
rulers in Judea, figure ominously in the biblical narratives
well known to Shakespeare's audience. Seeking to extir-
pate the threat Jesus' birth posed, Archelaus ordered the
death of all Judea's male children under two years old (see
Matthew 2, especially 7-16), and, similarly anxious about
his rule, Antipas ordered the execution of John the Baptist
(Matthew 14:1-11). The great medieval Corpus Christi
religious plays presented Herod Archelaus as the archetypal raging tyrant. Hamlet remembers him when he
warns the players against out-Heroding Herod, and he is
used by Henry V to threaten Harfleur's citizens: "the mad
mothers with their howls confused / Do break the clouds,

as did the wives of Jewry / At Herod's bloody-hunting slaughtermen" (*Henry V*, III.3). Shakespeare's audience might have made a still common mistake and collapsed the two later Herods into one, making a further strong connection among the play's threatening Herod, the medieval dramatic tyrant, Caesar Augustus's (the later title of the play's "Caesar") order for a census that brought Mary and Joseph to Bethlehem (according to the Gospel account), the birth of Jesus, and the flight of Mary, Joseph, and Jesus into Egypt to escape Herod Antipas's enmity. Herod of Jewry, whichever "Herod" the audience might imagine – the historical ones, the biblical ones, or a medieval dramatic one – provides a further, ominous signifier of cultural difference here.

Antony and Cleopatra dramatizes a deeply fraught moment in European history, one especially significant for Shakespeare's first audiences: the end of republican Rome, the beginning of imperial Rome, the confusing and to that audience hateful animosity of the Roman-sponsored administration in Judea toward Jesus' parents and their people, the soon-to-come moment of the Messiah. Cleopatra and her Egyptian monarchy were strange and threatening and puzzling; so too were the Judea and Jewry of Herod. History and culture, belief and prejudice make the moment of *Antony and Cleopatra* demanding for Shakespeare's audiences and later ones. As any great play must, *Antony and Cleopatra* presents these demands as acts and as human relations.

Learning that Antony has made a politically advantageous marriage to Caesar's sister Octavia, Cleopatra describes her Roman lover – now, it seems, her betrayer – as a visual puzzle, a combination of mythic female monster (Gorgon) and mythic male god of war (Mars): "Though he be painted one way like a Gorgon, / The other way's a Mars" (II.5.116–17). Agelessly unwithered, aging Cleopatra, the hero famously accorded "infinite variety" (II.2.246), a character "Whom everything becomes" (I.1.49), cannot herself still Antony's changes. Later,

Antony finds himself a "vapor" (IV.14.3) that "cannot hold this visible shape" (IV.14.14), a person or body as "indistinct / As water is in water" (IV.14.10–11). Authority melts from him even as his self-conception dissolves. Varying Cleopatra, unshaped Antony inhabit a drama that itself cannot easily be stilled.

Written about 1607, *Antony and Cleopatra* falls between the tragedies usually considered Shakespeare's greatest (*Hamlet, Othello, Lear, Macbeth*) and the tragicomedies (*Pericles, Cymbeline, The Winter's Tale, The Tempest*) that conclude his career. Just as its dramatic geography joins East and West, Egypt and Rome, *Antony and Cleopatra* bridges high tragedy and splendid comedy. Mixing verbal styles and seemingly contradictory emotions and dramatic events topsy-turvy, the play resists generic, emotional, and intellectual pigeonholes. It mixes and inverts male and female, queen, peasant, and triumvir, Egyptian, Roman, Jew, middle age and youth, political calculation, nostalgic reminiscence, present pleasure, future – even immortal – hope, a republic past and an empire to come.

Like *Romeo and Juliet* and *Troilus and Cressida,* the title of *Antony and Cleopatra* names two central characters who are lovers, but the earlier tragedies are very different. Profoundly influential family histories engulf the loving young couples of the earlier plays. Romeo and Juliet struggle against ancient family feud; Troilus and Cressida, whose separation is almost casually initiated by her traitor father's desire to be reunited with his daughter, try to establish their love amidst her uncle Pandarus's self-interested scheming and the political manipulations of Troilus's family and their advisers and against the antagonistic example of Helen and Paris. By contrast, Antony is regularly stripped – or strips himself – of family ties. First, his Roman warrior wife Fulvia dies; later he abandons his new wife, Octavia, when he is "nodded," as Caesar nastily says, back to Cleopatra. Antony occasionally uses both loss and abandonment as self-castigation or self-pity: trying to extort love from Cleopatra, for example, he will recall Octavia:

> Have I my pillow left unpressed in Rome,
> Forborne the getting of a lawful race,
> And by a gem of women, to be abused
> By one that looks on feeders?
>   (III.13.106-9)

But these moments seem more attitudinizing than deeply felt, occasions when Antony plays to an audience rather than reproaching himself. Neither Fulvia's death nor Octavia's abandonment finally influences his behavior. As the play portrays Cleopatra's family, it consists principally of her children; Caesar critically lists them as "Caesarion, whom they call my father's son, / And all the unlawful issue that their lust / Since then hath made between them" (III.6.6-8). Like Antony, Cleopatra uses her family and its loss as a form of rhetorical emphasis:

> From my cold heart let heaven engender hail
> . . . .
>   The next Caesarion smite,
> Till by degrees the memory of my womb,
> Together with my brave Egyptians all,
> By the discandying of this pelleted storm,
> Lie graveless. . . .
>   (III.13.159, 162-66)

The "next Caesarion" is Cleopatra's next male descendant, her future manchild, and his emotive significance here is dynastic, a future child subsumed in the lost memory of Cleopatra's line.

These passages, including Caesar's list, construe family ties as political, not personal, whereas the earlier two-hero tragedies generally show the family as separate from peripheral political interests (*Romeo and Juliet*) or (in *Troilus and Cressida*) as personally manipulated hooks upon which largely extra-familial war aims sometimes depend. Family becomes political when family members are themselves important political actors, as Antony and Cleopatra are, and Romeo, Juliet, Cressida, and Troilus are not. For Cleopatra, Caesar, and Antony family matters are political matters. Cleopatra and Antony act upon the world stage, and their actions consequently have or may have high tragic effects; the earlier lovers are almost exclusively involved in what would be, in another dramatic world, domestic comedy. Where the earlier tragedies kept the political and familial worlds relatively or even exclusively separate, *Antony and Cleopatra* mixes the genres of domestic-comedies-turned-tragedies (the earlier two plays) with world-shaking actions that are often represented as domestic comedy – tragedy-turned-comedy-turned-tragedy again.

Cleopatra and Antony are world actors who act foolishly, who simultaneously play both state tragedy and domestic comedy. Their actions, their political and military failures, remake the Mediterranean world, and their possible failure threatens to humiliate them before the Roman populace, as Antony fears (IV.14.72-77) and Cleopatra vividly imagines:

> Shall they hoist me up
> And show me to the shouting varletry
> Of censuring Rome?
> . . . .
> Saucy lictors
> Will catch at us like strumpets, and scald rhymers
> Ballad us out o' tune. . . .
> . . . .
> Antony
> Shall be brought drunken forth, and I shall see
> Some squeaking Cleopatra boy my greatness
> I' th' posture of a whore.
>   (V.2.55-57, 215-17, 219-22)

Strumpets and whores and drunks – Cleopatra, her court, her lover will become a scabby ("scald") joke about seduction, sexual obsession, and excess of all sorts.

In *Antony and Cleopatra,* the seesaw structure of the earlier two-hero tragedies (Montague/Capulet, Greek/Trojan) continues: Roman/Egyptian. The play may simplify itself into these national or racial or cultural dichotomies, and at first glance it seems easy to draw up a list. Thus, according to the Romans and some Egyptians some of the time, Rome represents honor and duty while Egypt is a place of distracting sensual pleasure. The conflicting pressures appear immediately in Antony's reaction to Fulvia's death (I.2.) and Caesar's self-interested tirade: "If," he says, Antony

>   filled
> His vacancy with his voluptuousness,
> Full surfeits and the dryness of his bones
> Call on him for't. But to confound such time
> That drums him from his sport and speaks as loud
> As his own state and ours, 'tis to be chid –
> As we rate boys who, being mature in knowledge,
> Pawn their experience to their present pleasure
> And so rebel to judgment.
>
>   (I.4.25-33)

Antony's and Caesar's "state" and the seriousness of the times demand only maturity, judgment, experience, not boyishly self-indulgent voluptuousness.

The conversion of family-feeling into politics, the political authority of the two central actors and their necessary sensitivity to scandal and public opinion sharply distinguish Cleopatra and Antony from Juliet, Cressida, Troilus, and Romeo. All these differences help define the special quality of *Antony and Cleopatra* as a two-hero drama. Still, it is Shakespeare's last play in this difficult tragic form, and – perhaps as an aging artist's venture? – it is a play whose lover-heroes are notably middle-aged and aware of time's passing and authority's ebb, aware of wrinkles, of gray hair, of fading sexual attractiveness.

The aging or the youthful human body becomes one of the play's most evocative battlegrounds. Though Caesar was historically twenty-three as the play opens, Cleopatra calls him "scarce-bearded" – world-sharing Caesar lacks a mature man's hairy chin. Cleopatra, who cheerfully (?) and attractively describes herself as "wrinkled deep in time," was historically thirty-eight, and Antony, who hopes he has the "spirit of a youth" even as he agrees his hair mingles white and brown, was fifty-two. Antony recalls Philippi, when he "struck / The lean and wrinkled Cassius" (III.11.36–37); himself wrinkled now, he must "To the young man," Caesar, "send humble treaties, dodge / And palter in the shifts of lowness" (III.11.62–63). Self-pityingly, he imagines that Caesar, who "wears the rose / Of youth upon him," requires Cleopatra to offer "this grizzled head" as the price of her freedom and, perhaps, sovereignty over her kingdom. Just as Caesar earlier portrayed Antony as an aging playboy, a *boy*, so Antony continues, "He calls me boy, and chides as he had power / To beat me out of Egypt" (IV.1.1–2). More significant than this schoolyard nastiness is Antony's sense of how time has passed and with it his physical endurance as well as his political greatness: Caesar, he admits, "seems / Proud and disdainful, harping on what I am, / Not what he knew I was" (III.13.141–43). "Not what he knew I was" powerfully states the passage of time, the loss of physical prowess and political authority. Most of all, it admits the loss of *dignity*.

Living in "such time / That drums him [Antony] from his sport and speaks as loud / As his own state and ours [Caesar's]" and mastering time are also Roman, not Egyptian, goals and, even more important, a Roman talent. Caesar ominously promises that "the time shall not / Outgo my thinking on" (III.2.60–61) Antony and his marriage to Octavia. Antony is at least momentarily grateful that Pompey's military adventures have so shaken the world: "The beds i' th' East are soft; and thanks to you, / That called me timelier than my purpose hither; / For I have gained by't" (II.6.50-52). As Antony's ambivalent balance between timeliness and a contrary untimely or ill-timed purpose suggests, the passage of time may also mark a movement from "Roman" to "Egyptian" behavior. When Caesar recalls Antony's past Roman greatness, it is in terms of hardship suffered, of endurance, as opposed to his present Egyptian "lascivious wassails."

Reveling on the banks of the Nile turns dutiful Roman soldiers into errant boys. It also turns men and boys into women:

> he fishes, drinks, and wastes
> The lamps of night in revel; is not more manlike
> Than Cleopatra, nor the queen of Ptolemy
> More womanly than he. . . .
>
> (I.4.4-7)

Even before Caesar voices his hostility, Enobarbus and Charmian have been momentarily confused over which leader is about to enter: "Hush, here comes Antony. / Not he, the queen" (I.2.78). Throughout the second half of the play, the interchange of meanings and values, purposes and desires between Cleopatra and Antony makes them, for themselves and for others, so intermingled that all find it difficult and perhaps not even necessary to distinguish queen and triumvir in terms of female and male.

The Roman way is very different, stringently separating man from boy, male from female, husband from wife. Where Caesar represents himself as both a model Roman and the defender of Roman values, he represents his sister Octavia as a model Roman wife and mother: she should "prove such a wife / As my thoughts make thee . . . the piece of virtue" (III.2.25-26, 28). An apparently "neutral" observer agrees Octavia is "of a holy, cold, and still conversation," and Cleopatra has to assault a messenger (II.5) to ensure he reports ill of Octavia's voice, stature, and appearance (III.3). Octavia plainly stands in dramaturgical opposition to Cleopatra, just as Cleopatra stands in opposition to Caesar, and Rome opposes Egypt. Between each pair – the play's ordering implies – Antony must choose, a middle-aged Prince Hal caught between his successful, stern-faced father (Henry IV/Caesar) and the joyously irresponsible failure, Falstaff/Cleopatra. Like his supposed ancestor Hercules, Antony stands at a crossroads where one path leads to heavenly Virtue, the other to hellish Vice. Rome, Caesar, marriage, and world domination one way; Egypt, Cleopatra, sensual indulgence, and political failure the other. Or so the play may be understood.

These classically elegant orderings of opposed tensions are no sooner hinted than they begin to fail and dissatisfy. The play throws many ambiguities over what seem its most persuasive and satisfying structures. There are so many ambiguities, in fact, that eventually we must accept their unsettling force as superior to the reassuring stasis of paired and tripled opposition.

Consider the frequent contrast of Egyptian extravagance and Roman restraint. Throughout the play we *hear* of Cleopatra's and Antony's excess: their first meeting, their transvestite sex games, their banquets, drunkenness, déclassé mock fights with "knaves," and so forth – an almost endless catalogue of rule-breaking. Yet those accounts are always *accounts*; they are reports transmitted to us, usually through a prejudiced Roman lens or, perhaps just as distorting, the romantic, now bittersweet memories of Antony and Cleopatra themselves. Antony proposes "one other gaudy night" (III.13.183) before what will prove his decisive naval defeat at Actium, and Cleopatra and Enobarbus recall many a midnight revel on the banks of the Nile. Yet the only "Egyptian bacchanals" (II.7.102) the play dramatizes – an all-male party where even cool Caesar's cheeks are "burnt" and his brain "grows fouler" with wine, where Lepidus, "the third part of the world," is "high-colored" and carried home helplessly drunk – is aboard Pompey's galley in Rome, not Egypt.

Before the grand, historically important figures have their bacchanal, their subordinates meet at arm's length. The men who actually do and suffer war's ugly business share their bottom-up views of high politics, high loves. One, Pompey's follower Menas, offers to kill his leader's enemies:

> These three world-sharers, these competitors,
> Are in thy vessel. Let me cut the cable;
> And when we are put off, fall to their throats.
> All there is thine.
>
> (II.7.69-72)

And Pompey, eager for dominion, fearful of dishonor, reluctantly demurs:

> Ah, this thou shouldst have done,
> And not have spoke on't. In me 'tis villainy;
> In thee't had been good service. Thou must know,
> 'Tis not my profit that does lead mine honor;
> Mine honor, it.
>
> (II.7.72-76)

Kill first, tell later. Profit, and victory, first; honor after. Does this little episode represent Roman honor or Egyptian treachery?

Before that dishonorable, clever victory forfeited, Antony's and Pompey's followers converse in a relaxed prelude to their leaders' meeting. Enobarbus explains Antony's fascination and seeming dereliction from Roman duty when he describes Cleopatra and Antony's first meeting:

> The barge she sat in, like a burnished throne,
> Burned on the water. The poop was beaten gold;
> Purple the sails, and so perfumèd that

> The winds were lovesick with them. The oars were
>   silver,
> Which to the tune of flutes kept stroke and made
> The water which they beat to follow faster,
> As amorous of their strokes. For her own person,
> It beggared all description. She did lie
> In her pavilion, cloth-of-gold of tissue,
> O'erpicturing that Venus where we see
> The fancy outwork nature. . . .
>
> (II.2.201–11)

And Enobarbus goes on.

In performance, there have been two main ways to deliver this speech: as awe or as smut. Performed one way, Cleopatra enthralls Enobarbus as Enobarbus says Cleopatra enthralled Antony – she surpasses painters' and sculptors' finest imaginings of Venus, the most beautiful goddess. Performed another way, Cleopatra is male fantasy, a sexy, disembodied lust icon, more appropriate for a poster than for worship. The so-called barge speech – and the choices it forces on the director – tells us at least as much about the speaker as about the scene and character he describes, as do so many other moments in the play.

Sexy, even raunchy (Shakespeare's word is "riggish"), Cleopatra undoubtedly is, but the play's joyous verbal celebration of sexuality begins with the Roman Enobarbus's wittily smutty "light answers" – Antony's rebuke of his subordinate's response to news that Antony's wife, Fulvia, "a great spirit," he says, has died. Jollying his despondent master and acknowledging Egypt's powerful attractions, Enobarbus makes ambivalent Roman jokes about "celerity in dying" (eager sexual climax), about "a wonderful piece of work" (Cleopatra, a wonder of the world of sexuality), about "the business you have broached here" in Egypt (both political "business" and the broaching or opening of Cleopatra's, "Egypt's," body). Once again, purportedly Egyptian qualities prove to be Roman. Enobarbus's ambivalence echoes the audience's. For Enobarbus, ambivalence leads to mortal heartbreak, when he is caught between pragmatic reasoning and idealistic emotion (IV.6): loyalty to Antony; a frank recognition of his weaknesses and the strong toils (as Caesar says, V.2.347) they both recognize in the "East"; an equally frank recognition of the military and political folly they both acknowledge, and Antony embraces.

As an element in the drama, Enobarbus sketches Antony's experiences at a less exalted level; he serves Antony (and Shakespeare) as Gloucester does Lear. Though she has far more numerous followers than Antony, Cleopatra has none who amplify her situation the way Enobarbus's words and acts do Antony's; indeed, some of the most revealing remarks about Antony come in Enobarbus's arguments with Cleopatra, arguments that manage to reveal little about her motives and purposes. For much of the play, Cleopatra is what others make of her. Brief, often magical, scenes in Egypt when Antony is away offer glimpses of her attitudes and values, but these episodes mostly "confirm" or extend the already hopelessly contradictory Roman views of her. The audience only begins to have some sort of direct experience of Cleopatra once Antony is dead. She hardly becomes "knowable," but the veil of Roman rancor and envy no longer so manifestly lies between audience and hero.

Shakespeare's unprecedented decision to remove so important a character as Antony with about one sixth of the play (all of Act V in modern editions) remaining – a dramaturgical gamble other Jacobean playwrights hardly ever dared – leaves the audience to watch Cleopatra's fashioning of her own death and, just as important, her refashioning of what Antony's life and death mean. Suddenly, interpretation – which earlier had arisen in the watching, commenting, reacting characters around the central couple – now falls first to the dying Antony, who bungles self-interpretation almost as badly as he botches suicide, and then to Cleopatra.

She says she "dreamt there was an emperor Antony," one whose

> legs bestrid the ocean; his reared arm
> Crested the world . . .
> . . . .
>   For his bounty,
> There was no winter in't: an Antony it was
> That grew the more by reaping. . . .
>   (V.2.83–84, 87–89)

When the stolid Roman Dolabella soberly denies Cleopatra's dream, he only elicits a grander – or is it only more grandiose? – vision of Antony:

> But if there be nor ever were one such,
> It's past the size of dreaming. Nature wants stuff
> To vie strange forms with fancy, yet t' imagine
> An Antony were nature's piece 'gainst fancy,
> Condemning shadows quite.
>   (V.2.97–101)

This comparison, in which Antony becomes nature's triumphant rebuke to the highest human artistic imaginings ("shadows"), recalls and then overgoes Enobarbus's claim that Cleopatra on her barge overpictured the painters' and sculptors' imagined Venus. Artists have fancies and Cleopatra first has a dream, but then her recalled Antony is past the size of dreaming and far beyond "fancy." The speech is one of Shakespeare's most powerful and successful "metadramatic" moments, since the claims of artistic (even human) transcendence are, of course, conveyed in his words and spoken by a most human actor.

Perhaps still more profound or desperate than Cleopatra's remaking of the Antony we have seen lurching among imagined selves, struggling simultaneously to retain a time-defying "Roman" martial greatness and to achieve a time-denying "Egyptian" greatness as Cleopatra's partner, is Cleopatra's further, concluding effort to supersede the very values through which the play has construed the meanings of Cleopatra and Antony. Or, since so much rests in the interpreting times, it might be better to say she seeks to refashion the play's celebrities represented as "Antony" and "Cleopatra" and their story.

Cleopatra's long dying is – she claims – after the high Roman fashion (IV.15.90): she melds in death Egypt and Rome. She will beat her Roman enemies at their own game, the game of dominating time, for time's passage inevitably ends in human death:

> My desolation does begin to make
> A better life. 'Tis paltry to be Caesar:
> Not being Fortune, he's but Fortune's knave,
> A minister of her will. And it is great
> To do that thing that ends all other deeds,
> Which shackles accidents and bolts up change;
> Which sleeps, and never palates more the dung,
> The beggar's nurse and Caesar's.
>
> (V.2.1–8)

The paradoxes are clear and not susceptible to logical "solution." Beggars and emperors all die, all suckle dung. We are all death's suitors. To end by suicide our common oppression does end accident and change, but how is it "great"? Or how may it be *made* great?

Antony's tentative answer was to be "A bridegroom in my death and run into't / As to a lover's bed" (IV.14.100-101). His run, however, proves an ungainly limp; defeated at sea and on land, Antony defeats himself and fails to commit an "appropriate" Roman suicide and lives long enough to know that he has been the apparent victim of another one of Cleopatra's love tricks – a clumsy sacrifice to farce. Cleopatra remakes Antony's failed *Liebestode* and offers the play's concluding emotional answer to the unanswerable: "I am again for Cydnus, / To meet Mark Antony." Dying, Antony supposed himself a bridegroom. Cleopatra finally goes further: "Husband, I come: / Now to that name my courage prove my title!"

A. R. BRAUNMULLER
University of California, Los Angeles

Note on Sources and Dates

SHAKESPEARE'S MAIN DOCUMENTARY source for *Antony and Cleopatra* was Thomas North's translation (from Amyot's earlier French translation) of Plutarch's *Lives of the Noble Grecians and Romanes* (1579 and later, expanded, editions). At several points in the play, Shakespeare closely versifies North's typically exuberant Elizabethan translation. Plutarch "paralleled" famous Greek and Roman personages; he joined Antony with Demetrius of Macedonia, another martial hero who had early success and final, military-political, failure. It seems likely that Shakespeare also knew in Latin, or French, or in Thomas Lodge's 1602 English translation, Flavius Josephus's *Antiquities of the Jews*. Cleopatra (she was typically the sole title character) was the subject of many Continental and English plays throughout the sixteenth century, and Shakespeare probably knew more than the title of one or more of these plays. For further details and generous extracts, see Geoffrey Bullough, *Narrative and Dramatic Sources of Shakespeare,* 8 vols. (New York: Columbia University Press, and London: Routledge, 1957-75), vol. V (1964).

Cleopatra was born in 69 B.C., Antony about 83 B.C.; both died in 30 B.C. Gaius Octavius (sometimes "Octavian" and regularly called "Caesar" in *Antony and Cleopatra*) became the first Roman emperor, Augustus, and died A.D. 14. The assassination of Julius Caesar in 44 B.C. led to the formation of a series of triumvirates, the last of which (Antony, Octavius Caesar, Lepidus) began in 43 B.C. and effectively collapsed in 36 B.C.; in the immediate aftermath of Julius Caesar's death, this triumvirate defeated Julius Caesar's principal assassins, Brutus and Cassius, at Philippi in 42 B.C. Fulvia was Antony's third wife and he her third husband; she died in 40 B.C. The play's

Pompey was the younger son of Pompey the Great and generally supported Antony against Octavius Caesar; the play depicts the Pact of Misenum (39 B.C.), but in the next year Octavius attacked Pompey's forces and eventually drove him to death by execution in Asia (36 B.C.). Octavius's decisive defeat of Antony occurred at sea near Actium in September 31 B.C. (compare *Antony and Cleopatra*, III.8-11), though the military struggle continued for a while longer.

Note on the Text

ANTONY AND CLEOPATRA was first published in the folio of 1623, apparently printed from Shakespeare's manuscript or from a transcription of it. Undivided into acts and scenes, the folio text lacks some important stage directions and includes "ghost" characters, confusing or inadequately distinguished character names, and other anomalies that might have been removed in a text fully prepared for production. The act/scene divisions in this edition are editorial, not original. The following list of departures from the folio attempts to list changes affecting interpretation; it omits typographical errors (i.e., those that do not produce a plausible word), uncontroversial modernizations, relineation, and places where speech prefixes and proper names have been standardized. The adopted reading (including speech prefixes – all are derived from the editorial tradition) appears in italics and is followed by the folio reading in roman.

I.1   18 *me!* me,   39 *On* One   50 *whose* who
I.2   39 *fertile* foretell   60 *Charmian* Alexas   79 *Saw* Save   109 *minds* windes   111 s.d. *a second* another   110 SECOND 1.   114, 115 THIRD (not in F)   137 *occasion* an occasion   178 *leave* love   183 *Hath* Have   194 *place is* places; *requires* require
I.3   20 *What,* What   24 *know —* know.   25 *betrayed* betrayèd   33 *sued* suèd   43 *services* Servicles   51 *thrived* thrivèd   80 *blood: No more.* blood no more?   82 *my* (not in F)
I.4   3 *Our* One   8 *Vouchsafed* vouchsafe   9 *the abstract* th' abstracts   21 *smell* smels   44 *deared* fear'd   46 *lackeying* lacking   47 SECOND (not in F)   49 *Make* Makes   56 *wassails* Vassailes   75 *we* me
I.5   5 *time* time: 29 *time?* time.   34 s.d. *Alexas* Alexas from Caesar   50   *dumbed* dumbe   61 *man* mans
II.1   2, 5 MENECRATES Mene.;   16, 18, 38 MENAS Mene.;   21 *waned* wand   41 *warred* wan'd   43 *greater.* greater,   44 *all,* all:
II.2   76–77 *you . . . Alexandria;* you, . . . Alexandria   113   *soldier* Souldier,   122–23 *staunch, . . . world* staunch . . . world: 128 *so* say   129 *reproof* proofe   130 *deserved* deservèd   155-56 *hand: / Further*

hand / Further   158 **s.d.** *[They clasp hands.]* (not in F)   180 **s.d.** *[Exe-unt.]* Exit omnes.   204 *lovesick with.* Love-sicke. / With   214 *glow* glove   216 *gentlewomen* Gentlewoman 233 *"no"* no; *heard* hard 238 *plowed* ploughèd   242 *And, breathless,* And breathlesse

II.3   8 *OCTAVIA* (not in F)   19 *high, unmatchable* high unmatchable   21 *afeard* a fear   23 *thee; no more but when to thee.* thee no more but: when to thee,   29 *away* alway

II.5   2 *ALL* Omnes   10–11 *river: there, / My . . . off,* River there / My . . . off.   12 *finned* fine   28 *him,* him.   43 *is* 'tis   96 *face, to me* face to me,   111 *Alexas;* Alexas   115 *not, Charmian,* not Charmian,

II.6   **s.d.** *Agrippa, with* Agrippa, Menas, with   19 *is* his   30 *present—how you take* present how you take)   39 *ANTONY . . . LEPIDUS* Omnes 43 *telling.* telling.   52 *gained* gainèd   58 *composition* composion   66 *meanings* meaning   69 *of* (not in F)   81 *CAESAR . . . LEPIDUS* All   81 **s.d.** *all but* Manet

II.7   16 **s.d.** *[and a Boy]* (not in F)   90 *is* he is   98 *grows* grow   100 *all; four days* all, foure dayes,   110 *bear* beate 112 *BOY [Sings.]* (not in F) 119 *off* of   123 *Splits* Spleet's   127 *father's* Father   128–29 *not. / Menas* not Menas

III.1   3 *body* body,   4 *army.* Army   5 *SILIUS* Romaine (throughout scene)

III.2   10 *AGRIPPA* Ant.   16 *figures* Figure   20 *beetle. [. . .] So—* Beetle, so: 49 *full* the full   59 *wept* weepe

III.3   18 *lookedst* look'st

III.4   8 *them* then   9 *took't* look't   24 *yours* your   30 *Your* You   38 *has* he's

III.5   12 *world* would; *hast* hadst; *chaps,* chaps   14 *the one* (not in F)

III.6   13 *he there proclaimed the kings* hither proclaimèd the King   19 *reported,* reported   22 *know* knowes   28 *triumvirate* Triumpherate   29 *being, that* being that,   72 *Manchus* Mauchus   79 *do* does

III.7   4 *it is* it it   5 *Is't not* If not,   20 *Canidius* Camidias   21 *Brundusium* Brandusium   23 *Toryne* Troine   35 *muleters* Militers   51 *Actium* Action   72 *CANIDIUS* Ven.   78 *Well* Well,   80 *in* with

III.8   6 **s.d.** *Exeunt* exit

III.10   **s.d.** *Enobarbus* Enobarbus and Scarus   14 *June* Inne   28 *he* his

III.11   6 *ALL* Omnes   19 *that* them   22 *pray,* pray   44 *He is* Hee's 47 *seize* cease   56 *followed* followèd   58 *tow* stowe   59 *Thy* The

III.13   10 *merèd* meered   26 *caparisons* comparisons   55 *Caesar* Caesars   57 *feared* fearèd   60 *deserved* deservèd   74 *this* this; *deputation* disputation,   90 *me. Of late,* me of late.   103 *again. This* againe, the 112–13 *eyes, / In . . . filth* eyes / In . . . filth,   132 *'a* a   137 *whipped for . . . him.* whipt. For . . . him,   162 *smite,* smile   165 *discandying* discandering   168 *sits* sets   178 *sinewed* sinewèd   199 *on* in   201 **s.d.** *Exit* Exeunt

IV.1   3 *combat,* combat.

IV.2   1 *No.* No?   12 *And thou* Thou   19 *ALL* Omnes

IV.3   7 *THIRD SOLDIER* 2   8 *FOURTH SOLDIER* 2   10 *THIRD SOLDIER* 1   15 *loved* lovèd   17, 22 *ALL* Omnes

IV.4 5–6 *too. / What's* too, Anthony. / What's 6 *ANTONY* (not in F) 8 *CLEOPATRA* (not in F) 24 *CAPTAIN* Alex. 32 *thee* thee. 33 *steel.* Steele,

IV.5 1, 3, 6 *SOLDIER* Eros 17 *Dispatch.* Dispatch 17 **s.d.** *Exeunt* Exit

IV.6 20 *more* mote 36 *do't, I feel.* doo't. I feele

IV.7 8 **s.d.** *far off* (in F after "heads," line 6)

IV.8 18 *My* Mine 23 *favoring* savouring 26 *Destroyed* Destroyèd

IV.12 4 *augurers* Auguries 9 **s.d.** *Alarum . . . sea fight* (in F before line 1) 10 *betrayed* betrayèd 21 *spanieled* pannelled

IV.13 10 *death.* death

IV.14 4 *towered* toward 10 *dislimns* dislimes 19 *Caesar* Caesars 77 *ensued* ensuèd 95 **s.d.** *Kills himself* (in F after line 93) 104 *ho* how 144 **s.d.** *Exeunt* Exit

IV.15 54 *lived the* lived. The 76 *e'en* in 86 *What, what!* What, what

V.1 **s.d.** *Maecenas* Menas 3 **s.d.** *DERCETUS* Decretas 5, 13, 19 *DERCETUS* Decretas (or "Dec.") 28 *AGRIPPA* Dol. 31 *AGRIPPA* Dola. 36 *followed* followèd 48 **s.d.** *Enter an Egyptian* (in F after "says," line 51) 53 *all she has,* all, she has 54 *intents desires* intents, desires, 59 *live* leave 68 **s.d.** *Exit* Exit Proculeius

V.2 **s.d.** (F adds *and Mardian*) 35 *You* Pro. [s.p.] You 56 *varletry* Varlotarie 66 *me* (not in F) 81 *O,* o' 105 *smites* suites 140 *valued* valewèd 152 *followed* followèd 184 *price* prize 217 *Ballad us out o'* Ballads us out a 224 *my* mine 318 *awry* away 319 **s.d.** *in.* in, and Dolabella. 325 *here! Charmian* here Charmian 341 *diadem* diadem; 342 *mistress;* Mistris 365 *Exeunt* Exeunt omnes

Antony and Cleopatra

[NAMES OF THE ACTORS

MARK ANTONY *(Marcus Antonius)*
CAESAR *(Octavius Caesar)* } triumvirs
M. AEMILIUS LEPIDUS
OCTAVIA, *sister to Caesar and wife to Antony*
ENOBARBUS *(Domitius Enobarbus)*
VENTIDIUS } *friends*
EROS *to Antony*
SCARUS
DERCETUS
DEMETRIUS
PHILO
CANIDIUS, *lieutenant-general to Antony*
MAECENAS
AGRIPPA
DOLABELLA } *friends to Caesar*
PROCULEIUS
THIDIAS
GALLUS
TAURUS, *lieutenant-general to Caesar*
POMPEY *(Sextus Pompeius)*
MENAS
MENECRATES } *friends to Pompey*
VARRIUS
ROMAN OFFICER UNDER VENTIDIUS
A SCHOOLMASTER, *Ambassador from Antony
to Caesar*
CLEOPATRA, *Queen of Egypt*

ALEXAS
MARDIAN
SELEUCUS
DIOMEDES   } *attendants on Cleopatra*
IRAS
CHARMIAN
A SOOTHSAYER
A CLOWN
OFFICERS, SOLDIERS, MESSENGERS, ATTENDANTS]

SCENE: *The Roman Empire*
*

Antony and Cleopatra

❧ **I.1.** *Enter Demetrius and Philo.*

PHILO
Nay, but this dotage of our general's   1
O'erflows the measure: those his goodly eyes
That o'er the files and musters of the war
Have glowed like plated Mars, now bend, now turn   4
The office and devotion of their view   5
Upon a tawny front. His captain's heart,   6
Which in the scuffles of great fights hath burst
The buckles on his breast, reneges all temper   8
And is become the bellows and the fan
To cool a gypsy's lust.   10
    Flourish. Enter Antony, Cleopatra, her Ladies, the
    train, with Eunuchs fanning her.
                  Look where they come:
Take but good note, and you shall see in him
The triple pillar of the world transformed   12
Into a strumpet's fool. Behold and see.   13
CLEOPATRA
If it be love indeed, tell me how much.
ANTONY
There's beggary in the love that can be reckoned.

I.1 Alexandria   1 *dotage* foolish affection   4 *plated* armored   5 *office* duty
6 *tawny front* brown (or suntanned: see I.5.28) face   8 *reneges* rejects; *temper*
moderation   10 *gypsy* (1) native of Egypt (where European Gypsies were er-
roneously thought to originate), (2) deceitful woman   10 s.d. *Flourish* musical fanfare (for a person of the highest authority); *train* retinue   12 *The
triple . . . world* one of the three "pillars" of the world (the others being Octavius Caesar and Lepidus)   13 *fool* dupe

CLEOPATRA
16   I'll set a bourn how far to be beloved.

ANTONY
17   Then must thou needs find out new heaven, new earth.
        Enter a Messenger.

MESSENGER
18   News, my good lord, from Rome.

ANTONY   Grates me! The sum.

CLEOPATRA
        Nay, hear them, Antony.
20   Fulvia perchance is angry; or who knows
21   If the scarce-bearded Caesar have not sent
        His powerful mandate to you, "Do this, or this;
23   Take in that kingdom, and enfranchise that.
        Perform't, or else we damn thee."

ANTONY   How, my love?

CLEOPATRA
        Perchance? Nay, and most like:
26   You must not stay here longer, your dismission
        Is come from Caesar; therefore hear it, Antony.
28   Where's Fulvia's process – Caesar's I would say – both?
        Call in the messengers. As I am Egypt's queen,
30   Thou blushest, Antony, and that blood of thine
31   Is Caesar's homager: else so thy cheek pays shame
        When shrill-tongued Fulvia scolds. The messengers!

ANTONY
        Let Rome in Tiber melt and the wide arch
34   Of the ranged empire fall! Here is my space,
        Kingdoms are clay; our dungy earth alike
        Feeds beast as man. The nobleness of life

sacrifices duty for love

---

16 *bourn* limit **17** *new . . . earth* (the phrase is biblical, describing the new
Jerusalem: see Isaiah 65:17 and Revelations 21:1–4) **18** *Grates . . . sum* it
annoys me; be brief **20** *Fulvia* Antony's wife **21** *scarce-bearded* hardly
grown up enough to have a beard (Caesar was twenty-three) **23** *Take in*
conquer; *enfranchise* set free **26** *dismission* discharge (from serving in Egypt)
28 *process* summons **31** *homager* subordinate; *else* or else **34** *ranged*
arranged in order (i.e., like an army)

its not
ß te right thing to do

Is to do thus, when such a mutual pair   37
And such a twain can do't, in which I bind,
On pain of punishment, the world to weet   39
We stand up peerless.   40

CLEOPATRA   Excellent falsehood!
Why did he marry Fulvia and not love her?
I'll seem the fool I am not. Antony   42
Will be himself.

ANTONY   But stirred by Cleopatra.
Now for the love of Love and her soft hours,   44
Let's not confound the time with conference harsh.   45
There's not a minute of our lives should stretch   46
Without some pleasure now. What sport tonight?

CLEOPATRA
Hear the ambassadors.

ANTONY   Fie, wrangling queen!
Whom everything becomes, to chide, to laugh,   49
To weep, whose every passion fully strives   50
To make itself, in thee, fair and admired.
No messenger but thine, and all alone
Tonight we'll wander through the streets and note
The qualities of people. Come, my queen;
Last night you did desire it. – Speak not to us.
      Exeunt [Antony and Cleopatra] with the train
      [and Messenger].

DEMETRIUS
Is Caesar with Antonius prized so slight?   56

PHILO
Sir, sometimes when he is not Antony
He comes too short of that great property   58
Which still should go with Antony.

---

37 *thus* (perhaps indicating an embrace; perhaps a general reference to their
way of life) 39 *weet* know 42 *the fool . . . not* i.e., foolish enough to believe
you 44 *Love . . . hours* (the hours were imagined as women serving Venus,
goddess of love) 45 *confound* (1) waste, (2) mix 46 *stretch* pass 49 *becomes* (1) is transformed into, (2) adorns, graces 50 *passion* mood 56
prized valued 58 *property* distinction

DEMETRIUS   I am full sorry
60   That he approves the common liar, who
       Thus speaks of him at Rome; but I will hope
       Of better deeds tomorrow. Rest you happy.   *Exeunt.*

                      *

   ❧ **I.2** *Enter Enobarbus, Lamprius, a Soothsayer,*
      Rannius, Lucillius, Charmian, Iras, Mardian the
      Eunuch, and Alexas.

CHARMIAN   Lord Alexas, sweet Alexas, most anything
2   Alexas, almost most absolute Alexas, where's the sooth-
       sayer that you praised so to th' queen? O that I knew
4   this husband which, you say, must change his horns
       with garlands!
ALEXAS   Soothsayer!
SOOTHSAYER   Your will?
CHARMIAN   Is this the man? Is't you, sir, that know
       things?
SOOTHSAYER
10   In nature's infinite book of secrecy
       A little I can read.
ALEXAS   Show him your hand.
ENOBARBUS
       Bring in the banquet quickly; wine enough
       Cleopatra's health to drink.
CHARMIAN   Good sir, give me good fortune.
SOOTHSAYER
       I make not, but foresee.
CHARMIAN   Pray then, foresee me one.
SOOTHSAYER
       You shall be yet far fairer than you are.

---

60 *approves* confirms
    I.2 Alexandria **s.d.** *Enter Enobarbus . . . Alexas* (thus in folio, but Lam-
prius [who may be "a Soothsayer"], Rannius, and Lucillius are mute here and
do not appear elsewhere)   **2** *absolute* perfect   **4–5** *must . . . garlands* trade a
wedding wreath for a cuckold's traditional symbol, horns on the forehead (?)

CHARMIAN   He means in flesh.   19
IRAS   No, you shall paint when you are old.   20
CHARMIAN   Wrinkles forbid!
ALEXAS   Vex not his prescience, be attentive.
CHARMIAN   Hush!
SOOTHSAYER
  You shall be more beloving than beloved.
CHARMIAN   I had rather heat my liver with drinking.   25
ALEXAS   Nay, hear him.
CHARMIAN   Good now, some excellent fortune. Let me
  be married to three kings in a forenoon and widow
  them all. Let me have a child at fifty, to whom Herod   29
  of Jewry may do homage. Find me to marry me with   30
  Octavius Caesar, and companion me with my mistress.   31
SOOTHSAYER
  You shall outlive the lady whom you serve.
CHARMIAN   O excellent! I love long life better than figs.   33
SOOTHSAYER
  You have seen and proved a fairer former fortune   34
  Than that which is to approach.
CHARMIAN   Then belike my children shall have no names.   36
  Prithee, how many boys and wenches must I have?   37
SOOTHSAYER
  If every of your wishes had a womb,
  And fertile every wish, a million.
CHARMIAN   Out, fool! I forgive thee for a witch.   40
ALEXAS   You think none but your sheets are privy to your   41
  wishes.
CHARMIAN   Nay, come, tell Iras hers.
ALEXAS   We'll know all our fortunes.

---

19 *He . . . flesh* he means that you will put on weight   25 *liver* (the organ regarded as the seat of love)   29 *Herod* (an anachronistic reference to Herod
Archelaus, who massacred the infant boys of Judea and became an archetypal
tyrant in English drama)   31 *companion me with* make me equal to   33 *figs*
(figs were a slang analogue of penis and testicles)   34 *proved* experienced
36 *have no names* i.e., have no names derived from fathers   37 *wenches* girls
40 *I . . . witch* i.e., I can see that you have no prophetic powers   41 *privy to*
in on the secret of

ENOBARBUS   Mine, and most of our fortunes tonight, shall be drunk to bed.

IRAS   There's a palm presages chastity, if nothing else.

CHARMIAN   E'en as the o'erflowing Nilus presageth famine.

50   IRAS   Go, you wild bedfellow, you cannot soothsay.

51   CHARMIAN   Nay, if an oily palm be not a fruitful prognostication, I cannot scratch mine ear. – Prithee tell her but a workaday fortune.

SOOTHSAYER   Your fortunes are alike.

IRAS   But how, but how? Give me particulars.

SOOTHSAYER   I have said.

IRAS   Am I not an inch of fortune better than she?

CHARMIAN   Well, if you were but an inch of fortune better than I, where would you choose it?

60   IRAS   Not in my husband's nose.

CHARMIAN   Our worser thoughts heavens mend! Alexas – come, his fortune, his fortune. O, let him

63   marry a woman that cannot go, sweet Isis, I beseech thee, and let her die too, and give him a worse, and let worse follow worse till the worst of all follow him laughing to his grave, fiftyfold a cuckold. Good Isis, hear me this prayer, though thou deny me a matter of more weight; good Isis, I beseech thee.

IRAS   Amen, dear goddess, hear that prayer of the people.

70   For, as it is a heartbreaking to see a handsome man

71   loose-wived, so it is a deadly sorrow to behold a foul

72   knave uncuckolded. Therefore, dear Isis, keep decorum, and fortune him accordingly.

CHARMIAN   Amen.

ALEXAS   Lo now, if it lay in their hands to make me a cuckold, they would make themselves whores but

77   they'd do't.

---

51 *oily palm* sweaty hand (thought to indicate sensuality)   **51–52** *fruitful prognostication* prophetic sign of fertility   **60** (Iras prefers a long penis to a long nose)   **63** *go* have sexual intercourse; *Isis* Egyptian goddess of earth, fertility, and the moon   **71** *loose-wived* married to an unfaithful wife   **72–73** *keep decorum* i.e., act as suits his quality (see V.2.17 n.)

Enter Cleopatra.

ENOBARBUS

Hush, here comes Antony.

CHARMIAN   Not he, the queen.

CLEOPATRA

Saw you my lord?

ENOBARBUS   No, lady.

CLEOPATRA   Was he not here?

CHARMIAN   No, madam.   *80*

CLEOPATRA

He was disposed to mirth; but on the sudden

A Roman thought hath struck him. Enobarbus!   *82*

ENOBARBUS   Madam?

CLEOPATRA

Seek him, and bring him hither. Where's Alexas?

ALEXAS

Here at your service. My lord approaches.

Enter Antony with a Messenger.

CLEOPATRA

We will not look upon him. Go with us.

                    Exeunt [all but Antony and the Messenger].

MESSENGER

Fulvia thy wife first came into the field.

ANTONY

Against my brother Lucius?

MESSENGER   Ay.

But soon that war had end, and the time's state   *90*

Made friends of them, jointing their force 'gainst Caesar,

Whose better issue in the war from Italy   *92*

Upon the first encounter drave them.   *93*

ANTONY   Well, what worst?

MESSENGER

The nature of bad news infects the teller.

---

77 s.d. (the folio places Cleopatra's entrance here and performances explain
Enobarbus's mistake as sincere or ironic; alternatively, Cleopatra may enter
after "Not he, the queen")   82 *Roman thought* sobering (?) consideration of
duty   90 *time's state* conditions of the moment   92 *issue* success   93 *drave*
drove (a northern English word form)

ANTONY
     When it concerns the fool or coward. On.
     Things that are past are done with me. 'Tis thus:
     Who tells me true, though in his tale lie death,
98   I hear him as he flattered.
MESSENGER   Labienus –
     This is stiff news – hath with his Parthian force
100 Extended Asia: from Euphrates,
     His conquering banner shook, from Syria
     To Lydia and to Ionia,
     Whilst –
ANTONY   Antony, thou wouldst say.
MESSENGER   O, my lord.
ANTONY
104 Speak to me home, mince not the general tongue,
     Name Cleopatra as she is called in Rome;
     Rail thou in Fulvia's phrase, and taunt my faults
107 With such full license as both truth and malice
     Have power to utter. O, then we bring forth weeds
109 When our quick minds lie still, and our ills told us
110 Is as our earing. Fare thee well awhile.
MESSENGER
     At your noble pleasure.   *Exit Messenger.*
          Enter [a Second] Messenger.
ANTONY
     From Sicyon, how the news? Speak there!
SECOND MESSENGER
     The man from Sicyon –
ANTONY   Is there such a one?
SECOND MESSENGER
114 He stays upon your will.

---

98 *as* as if; *Labienus* Quintus Labienus, who had been sent by Brutus and
Cassius to seek aid against Antony and Octavius Caesar from Orodes, King
of Parthia, and was now commanding a Parthian army   100 *Extended* seized
104 *home* plainly; *mince . . . tongue* don't soften what everybody is saying
107 *license* freedom   109 *quick* live, fertile   110 *earing* being plowed (to
uproot the weeds)   114 *stays upon* waits

ANTONY   Let him appear.
  These strong Egyptian fetters I must break
  Or lose myself in dotage.

realizes his love

    Enter another Messenger, with a letter.
                  What are you?

THIRD MESSENGER
  Fulvia thy wife is dead.

ANTONY   Where died she?

THIRD MESSENGER
  In Sicyon.
  Her length of sickness, with what else more serious
  Importeth thee to know, this bears.   120
    [Gives a letter.]

ANTONY   Forbear me.
                [Exit Messenger.]
  There's a great spirit gone! Thus did I desire it.
  What our contempts doth often hurl from us,
  We wish it ours again. The present pleasure,
  By revolution lowering, does become   124
  The opposite of itself: she's good, being gone;
  The hand could pluck her back that shoved her on.
  I must from this enchanting queen break off: 127
  Ten thousand harms, more than the ills I know,
  My idleness doth hatch.
    Enter Enobarbus.
  How now, Enobarbus!   130

ENOBARBUS   What's your pleasure, sir?

ANTONY   I must with haste from hence.

ENOBARBUS   Why, then we kill all our women. We see
  how mortal an unkindness is to them: if they suffer our
  departure, death's the word.

ANTONY   I must be gone.

---

120 *Importeth* concerns; *Forbear* leave   **124** *By revolution lowering* i.e., moving downward on the revolving wheel of our opinions   **127** *enchanting* (Roman speakers often attribute magical powers to Cleopatra)

ENOBARBUS   Under a compelling occasion let women
138   die. It were pity to cast them away for nothing, though
between them and a great cause they should be es-
140   teemed nothing. Cleopatra, catching but the least noise
of this, dies instantly; I have seen her die twenty times
142   upon far poorer moment. I do think there is mettle in
death, which commits some loving act upon her, she
hath such a celerity in dying.

ANTONY   She is cunning past man's thought.

ENOBARBUS   Alack, sir, no; her passions are made of
nothing but the finest part of pure love. We cannot call
her winds and waters sighs and tears; they are greater
storms and tempests than almanacs can report. This
150   cannot be cunning in her; if it be, she makes a shower
151   of rain as well as Jove.

ANTONY   Would I had never seen her!

ENOBARBUS   O, sir, you had then left unseen a wonderful
piece of work, which not to have been blest withal
would have discredited your travel.

ANTONY   Fulvia is dead.

ENOBARBUS   Sir?

ANTONY   Fulvia is dead.

ENOBARBUS   Fulvia?

160   ANTONY   Dead.

ENOBARBUS   Why, sir, give the gods a thankful sacrifice.
When it pleaseth their deities to take the wife of a man
163   from him, it shows to man the tailors of the earth; com-
forting therein, that when old robes are worn out, there
165   are members to make new. If there were no more women
but Fulvia, then had you indeed a cut, and the case to be
lamented. This grief is crowned with consolation, your
old smock brings forth a new petticoat, and indeed the
tears live in an onion that should water this sorrow.

---

138 *die* (1) cease to exist, (2) Elizabethan slang for "have orgasm," a meaning
repeated in *die, dies, die,* and *dying* (138, 141, 144)   142 *moment* cause; *met-*
tle vigor   150 *makes* manufactures   151 *Jove* i.e., Jupiter Pluvius, Roman
god of rain   163 *the tailors* i.e., that the gods are the tailors   165 *members*
i.e., male sexual organs; *cut* and *case* (166) are slang for female genitalia

ANTONY
   The business she hath broachèd in the state   170
   Cannot endure my absence.
ENOBARBUS   And the business you have broached here   172
   cannot be without you; especially that of Cleopatra's,
   which wholly depends on your abode.   174
ANTONY
   No more light answers. Let our officers
   Have notice what we purpose. I shall break   176
   The cause of our expedience to the queen   177
   And get her leave to part. For not alone
   The death of Fulvia, with more urgent touches,   179
   Do strongly speak to us, but the letters too   *180*
   Of many our contriving friends in Rome   181
   Petition us at home. Sextus Pompeius   182
   Hath given the dare to Caesar and commands
   The empire of the sea. Our slippery people,
   Whose love is never linked to the deserver
   Till his deserts are past, begin to throw   186
   Pompey the Great and all his dignities
   Upon his son; who – high in name and power,
   Higher than both in blood and life – stands up   189
   For the main soldier; whose quality, going on,   190
   The sides o' th' world may danger. Much is breeding,   191
   Which, like the courser's hair, hath yet but life   192
   And not a serpent's poison. Say, our pleasure,
   To such whose place is under us, requires   194
   Our quick remove from hence.
ENOBARBUS   I shall do't.   *Exeunt.*

*

---

170 *broachèd* opened up **172** *business . . . broached* i.e., the sex acts you
have entered upon **174** *abode* staying **176** *break* tell **177** *expedience* ex-
pedition **179** *touches* motives **181** *contriving* i.e., acting in my interest
182 *at home* to return home; *Sextus Pompeius* son of Pompey the Great, now
(after Julius Caesar's death) a pirate **186** *throw* transfer **189** *blood and life*
vital energy **190** *going on* evolving **191** *danger* endanger **192** *courser's*
hair (horsehairs in water were thought to come to life as small serpents)
194 *place* rank

～ **I.3** *Enter Cleopatra, Charmian, Alexas, and Iras.*

CLEOPATRA
  Where is he?
CHARMIAN   I did not see him since.
CLEOPATRA
  See where he is, who's with him, what he does.
3   I did not send you. If you find him sad,
  Say I am dancing; if in mirth, report
  That I am sudden sick. Quick, and return.
                                    [Exit Alexas.]
CHARMIAN
  Madam, methinks if you did love him dearly,
  You do not hold the method to enforce
8   The like from him.
CLEOPATRA   What should I do, I do not?
CHARMIAN
  In each thing give him way, cross him in nothing.
CLEOPATRA
10   Thou teachest like a fool – the way to lose him!
CHARMIAN
11   Tempt him not so too far. I wish, forbear.
  In time we hate that which we often fear.
    Enter Antony.
13   But here comes Antony.
CLEOPATRA   I am sick and sullen.
ANTONY
14   I am sorry to give breathing to my purpose –
CLEOPATRA
  Help me away, dear Charmian! I shall fall.
16   It cannot be thus long; the sides of nature
  Will not sustain it.
ANTONY   Now, my dearest queen –

I.3 Alexandria   **3** *sad* serious   **8** *I do not* that I am not doing   **11** *Tempt* try;
I wish I wish you would   **13** *sullen* melancholy   **14** *breathing* utterance   **16**
sides of nature human body

CLEOPATRA
    Pray you stand farther from me.
ANTONY   What's the matter?
CLEOPATRA
    I know by that same eye there's some good news.
    What, says the married woman you may go?   20
    Would she had never given you leave to come!
    Let her not say 'tis I that keep you here.
    I have no power upon you; hers you are.
ANTONY
    The gods best know –
CLEOPATRA   O, never was there queen
    So mightily betrayed! Yet at the first
    I saw the treasons planted.
ANTONY   Cleopatra –
CLEOPATRA
    Why should I think you can be mine and true –
    Though you in swearing shake the thrònèd gods –
    Who have been false to Fulvia? Riotous madness,
    To be entangled with those mouth-made vows   30
    Which break themselves in swearing.
ANTONY   Most sweet queen –
CLEOPATRA
    Nay, pray you seek no color for your going,   32
    But bid farewell and go. When you sued staying,   33
    Then was the time for words: no going then,
    Eternity was in our lips and eyes,
    Bliss in our brows' bent; none our parts so poor   36
    But was a race of heaven. They are so still,   37
    Or thou, the greatest soldier of the world,
    Art turned the greatest liar.
ANTONY   How now, lady?

---

20 *the married woman* i.e., Fulvia   **32** *color* pretext   **33** *sued* begged for   **36** *bent* curve   **37** *a race of heaven* of heavenly origin; perhaps also "of heavenly flavor"

CLEOPATRA

40 I would I had thy inches; thou shouldst know
41 There were a heart in Egypt.

ANTONY   Hear me, queen:
    The strong necessity of time commands
    Our services awhile, but my full heart
44 Remains in use with you. Our Italy
45 Shines o'er with civil swords; Sextus Pompeius
    Makes his approaches to the port of Rome;
    Equality of two domestic powers
48 Breed scrupulous faction; the hated, grown to strength,
    Are newly grown to love; the condemned Pompey,
50 Rich in his father's honor, creeps apace
    Into the hearts of such as have not thrived
52 Upon the present state, whose numbers threaten;
53 And quietness, grown sick of rest, would purge
54 By any desperate change. My more particular,
55 And that which most with you should safe my going,
    Is Fulvia's death.

CLEOPATRA
    Though age from folly could not give me freedom,
    It does from childishness. Can Fulvia die?

ANTONY
    She's dead, my queen.
60 Look here, and at thy sovereign leisure read
61 The garboils she awaked. At the last, best,
    See when and where she died.

CLEOPATRA   O most false love!
63 Where be the sacred vials thou shouldst fill
    With sorrowful water? Now I see, I see,
    In Fulvia's death how mine received shall be.

---

41 *Egypt* i.e., both Cleopatra and her sovereign state 44 *in . . . you* for you to keep and use 45 *civil swords* i.e., civil war 48 *scrupulous faction* contest over trifles 52 *state* government 53–54 *grown . . . change* i.e., ill through peace, would cure itself by letting blood 54 *particular* personal concern 55 *safe* secure 61 *garboils* disturbances; *best* best news of all 63–64 *sacred vials . . . water* (a reference to the practice of consecrating bottles of tears to the dead)

ANTONY
 Quarrel no more, but be prepared to know
 The purposes I bear, which are, or cease,
 As you shall give th' advice. By the fire   68
 That quickens Nilus' slime, I go from hence   69
 Thy soldier, servant, making peace or war   70
 As thou affects.   71
CLEOPATRA   Cut my lace, Charmian, come –
 But let it be, I am quickly ill, and well –
 So Antony loves.   73
ANTONY   My precious queen, forbear,
 And give true evidence to his love, which stands 74
 An honorable trial.   75
CLEOPATRA   So Fulvia told me.
 I prithee turn aside and weep for her;
 Then bid adieu to me and say the tears
 Belong to Egypt. Good now, play one scene
 Of excellent dissembling, and let it look
 Like perfect honor.   80
ANTONY   You'll heat my blood. No more!
CLEOPATRA
 You can do better yet; but this is meetly.   81
ANTONY
 Now by my sword –   82
CLEOPATRA   And target. Still he mends.
 But this is not the best. Look, prithee, Charmian,
 How this Herculean Roman does become   84
 The carriage of his chafe.
ANTONY
 I'll leave you, lady.

---

68 *fire* i.e., the sun 69 *quickens* vivifies; *Nilus' slime* fertile mud left by the Nile's annual overflow 70 *servant* both vassal and lover 71 *affects* choosest; *lace* i.e., the fastenings that hold clothing close to her heart and lungs 73 *So* provided that; *forbear* desist 74 *stands* will sustain 75 *told* taught (Cleopatra ironically comments on how faithful Antony was to Fulvia) 81 *meetly* well suited 82 *target* shield 84–85 *How . . . chafe* i.e., how becomingly he plays his role of angry Hercules (from whom Antony supposedly descended)

CLEOPATRA   Courteous lord, one word.
    Sir, you and I must part, but that's not it;
    Sir, you and I have loved, but there's not it:
    That you know well. Something it is I would –
90 O, my oblivion is a very Antony,
91 And I am all forgotten.
ANTONY   But that your royalty
    Holds idleness your subject, I should take you
    For idleness itself.
CLEOPATRA   'Tis sweating labor
    To bear such idleness so near the heart
    As Cleopatra this. But, sir, forgive me,
96 Since my becomings kill me when they do not
97 Eye well to you. Your honor calls you hence;
    Therefore be deaf to my unpitied folly,
    And all the gods go with you. Upon your sword
100 Sit laurel victory, and smooth success
    Be strewed before your feet!
ANTONY   Let us go. Come:
    Our separation so abides and flies
    That thou residing here goes yet with me,
    And I hence fleeting here remain with thee.
    Away!   *Exeunt.*

                          *

 ∾ I.4 *Enter Octavius [Caesar], reading a letter, Lepidus,*
       and their train.

CAESAR
    You may see, Lepidus, and henceforth know
    It is not Caesar's natural vice to hate
3   Our great competitor. From Alexandria
    This is the news: he fishes, drinks, and wastes

---

90 *my . . . Antony* my forgetfulness is like Antony, who is now leaving (i.e.,
forgetting) me   91 *I . . . forgotten* (1) I have forgotten what I was going to
say, (2) I am all forgotten by Antony   91–92 *But . . . subject* if you were not
the queen of trifling   96 *my becomings* (1) those things that grace me, (2) my
changes (see I.1.49)   97 *Eye* look
I.4 Rome   3 *competitor* partner

The lamps of night in revel; is not more manlike
Than Cleopatra, nor the queen of Ptolemy   6
More womanly than he; hardly gave audience, or   7
Vouchsafed to think he had partners. You shall find there
A man who is the abstract of all faults   9
That all men follow.

LEPIDUS   I must not think there are
Evils enow to darken all his goodness: 11
His faults in him seem as the spots of heaven,   12
More fiery by night's blackness; hereditary
Rather than purchased, what he cannot change   14
Than what he chooses.

CAESAR
You are too indulgent. Let's grant it is not
Amiss to tumble on the bed of Ptolemy,
To give a kingdom for a mirth, to sit
And keep the turn of tippling with a slave,   19
To reel the streets at noon, and stand the buffet   20
With knaves that smell of sweat. Say this becomes him –
As his composure must be rare indeed   22
Whom these things cannot blemish – yet must Antony
No way excuse his foils when we do bear   24
So great weight in his lightness. If he filled
His vacancy with his voluptuousness,   26
Full surfeits and the dryness of his bones   27
Call on him for't. But to confound such time   28
That drums him from his sport and speaks as loud
As his own state and ours, 'tis to be chid –   30
As we rate boys who, being mature in knowledge,   31

---

6 *Ptolemy* Cleopatra's dead brother and husband   7 *audience* i.e., to Caesar's
messengers (cf. I.1)   9 *abstract* epitome   11 *enow* enough   12–13 *His ...
blackness* i.e., just as stars seem brighter against night's darkness, so Antony's
faults contrast with his virtues   14 *purchased* acquired   19 *keep ... of* take
turns   20 *stand the buffet* trade blows   22 *his composure* that man's character
24 *foils* disgraces   24–25 *when ... lightness* when his levity puts so heavy a
burden upon us   26 *vacancy* leisure   27–28 *Full ... him* i.e., let his own
physical symptoms be the reckoning   28 *confound* frustrate, waste   30
his ... ours his and our greatness   31 *rate* berate; *mature in knowledge* old
enough to know better

Pawn their experience to their present pleasure
33 And so rebel to judgment.
    Enter a Messenger.

LEPIDUS   Here's more news.

MESSENGER
    Thy biddings have been done and every hour,
    Most noble Caesar, shalt thou have report
    How 'tis abroad. Pompey is strong at sea,
    And it appears he is beloved of those
    That only have feared Caesar: to the ports
39   The discontents repair, and men's reports
40   Give him much wronged.

CAESAR   I should have known no less.
41   It hath been taught us from the primal state
    That he which is was wished until he were;
    And the ebbed man, ne'er loved till ne'er worth love,
44   Comes deared by being lacked. This common body,
45   Like to a vagabond flag upon the stream,
46   Goes to and back, lackeying the varying tide
    To rot itself with motion.
    [Enter a Second Messenger.]

SECOND MESSENGER   Caesar, I bring thee word
    Menecrates and Menas, famous pirates,
    Make the sea serve them, which they ear and wound
50   With keels of every kind. Many hot inroads
    They make in Italy; the borders maritime
52   Lack blood to think on't, and flush youth revolt.
    No vessel can peep forth but 'tis as soon
54   Taken as seen; for Pompey's name strikes more
    Than could his war resisted.

CAESAR   Antony,
56   Leave thy lascivious wassails. When thou once

---

33 *to* against   39 *discontents* discontented   40 *Give* declare   41 *from . . . state* since human history began (i.e., the creation of the world)   44 *Comes deared* becomes beloved; *common body* common people   45 *flag* iris (a flower)   46 *lackeying* following obsequiously (as a servant might)   52 *Lack blood* grow pale; *flush* vigorous   54–55 *strikes . . . resisted* is more effective than his forces would be if opposed   56 *wassails* carousings

Was beaten from Modena, where thou slew'st
Hirtius and Pansa, consuls, at thy heel
Did famine follow, whom thou fought'st against,
Though daintily brought up, with patience more   60
Than savages could suffer. Thou didst drink
The stale of horses and the gilded puddle   62
Which beasts would cough at. Thy palate then did deign   63
The roughest berry on the rudest hedge.
Yea, like the stag when snow the pasture sheets,
The barks of trees thou browsed. On the Alps
It is reported thou didst eat strange flesh,
Which some did die to look on. And all this –
It wounds thine honor that I speak it now –
Was borne so like a soldier that thy cheek   70
So much as lanked not.   71
LEPIDUS   'Tis pity of him.
CAESAR
Let his shames quickly
Drive him to Rome. 'Tis time we twain
Did show ourselves i' th' field; and to that end
Assemble we immediate council. Pompey
Thrives in our idleness.
LEPIDUS   Tomorrow, Caesar,
I shall be furnished to inform you rightly
Both what by sea and land I can be able   78
To front this present time.   79
CAESAR   Till which encounter,
It is my business too. Farewell.   80
LEPIDUS
Farewell, my lord. What you shall know meantime
Of stirs abroad, I shall beseech you, sir,
To let me be partaker.
CAESAR   Doubt not, sir;
I knew it for my bond.   *Exeunt.*   84

*

62 *stale* urine; *gilded* yellow-colored   63 *deign* accept   71 *lanked*
thinned   78 *be able* muster   79 *front* confront   84 *bond* duty

∾ **I.5** *Enter Cleopatra, Charmian, Iras, and Mardian.*

CLEOPATRA   Charmian!
CHARMIAN   Madam?
CLEOPATRA
3   Ha, ha. Give me to drink mandragora.
CHARMIAN   Why, madam?
CLEOPATRA
    That I might sleep out this great gap of time
    My Antony is away.
CHARMIAN   You think of him too much.
CLEOPATRA
    O, 'tis treason!
CHARMIAN   Madam, I trust, not so.
CLEOPATRA
    Thou, eunuch Mardian!
MARDIAN   What's your highness' pleasure?
CLEOPATRA
    Not now to hear thee sing. I take no pleasure
10   In aught an eunuch has. 'Tis well for thee
11   That, being unseminared, thy freer thoughts
12   May not fly forth of Egypt. Hast thou affections?
MARDIAN   Yes, gracious madam.
CLEOPATRA   Indeed?
MARDIAN
    Not in deed, madam; for I can do nothing
    But what indeed is honest to be done:
    Yet have I fierce affections, and think
    What Venus did with Mars.
CLEOPATRA   O Charmian,
    Where think'st thou he is now? Stands he, or sits he?
20   Or does he walk? Or is he on his horse?
21   O happy horse, to bear the weight of Antony!

_____

I.5 Alexandria 3 *Ha, ha* (an ambiguous and conventional phrase, perhaps indicating a yawn); *mandragora* mandrake (a drug) 11 *unseminared* castrated 12 *affections* desires 21 *O . . . Antony* (Cleopatra bawdily equates riding with sexual intercourse)

Do bravely, horse! For wot'st thou whom thou mov'st?   22
The demi-Atlas of this earth, the arm   23
And burgonet of men. He's speaking now,   24
Or murmuring, "Where's my serpent of old Nile?"
For so he calls me. Now I feed myself
With most delicious poison. Think on me
That am with Phoebus' amorous pinches black   28
And wrinkled deep in time. Broad-fronted Caesar,   29
When thou wast here above the ground, I was   30
A morsel for a monarch; and great Pompey
Would stand and make his eyes grow in my brow;
There would he anchor his aspect, and die   33
With looking on his life.
        Enter Alexas.
ALEXAS   Sovereign of Egypt, hail!
CLEOPATRA
How much unlike art thou Mark Antony!
Yet, coming from him, that great medicine hath   36
With his tinct gilded thee.
How goes it with my brave Mark Antony?   38
ALEXAS
Last thing he did, dear queen,
He kissed – the last of many doubled kisses –   40
This orient pearl. His speech sticks in my heart.   41
CLEOPATRA
Mine ear must pluck it thence.
ALEXAS   "Good friend," quoth he,
"Say the firm Roman to great Egypt sends   43
This treasure of an oyster; at whose foot,
To mend the petty present, I will piece
Her opulent throne with kingdoms. All the East,
Say thou, shall call her mistress." So he nodded,

---

22 *wot'st* knowest 23 *demi-Atlas* half-Atlas (i.e., Antony and Caesar jointly
hold up the world, as the god Atlas alone legendarily did) 24 *burgonet* helmet 28 *Phoebus* the sun 29 *Broad-fronted* wide-browed; *Caesar* Julius
Caesar 33 *aspect* gaze 36–37 *that . . . thee* (Cleopatra compares Antony to
the alchemists' great medicine that turned baser metals to gold) 38 *brave*
splendid 41 *orient* lustrous 43 *firm* constant

48   And soberly did mount an arm-gaunt steed,
      Who neighed so high that what I would have spoke
50   Was beastly dumbed by him.
CLEOPATRA   What was he, sad or merry?
ALEXAS
      Like to the time o' th' year between the extremes
      Of hot and cold, he was nor sad nor merry.
CLEOPATRA
      O well-divided disposition! Note him,
      Note him, good Charmian, 'tis the man; but note him.
      He was not sad, for he would shine on those
56   That make their looks by his; he was not merry,
      Which seemed to tell them his remembrance lay
      In Egypt with his joy; but between both.
      O heavenly mingle! Be'st thou sad or merry,
60   The violence of either thee becomes,
61   So does it no man else. – Met'st thou my posts?
ALEXAS
62   Ay, madam, twenty several messengers.
      Why do you send so thick?
CLEOPATRA   Who's born that day
      When I forget to send to Antony
      Shall die a beggar. Ink and paper, Charmian.
      Welcome, my good Alexas. Did I, Charmian,
      Ever love Caesar so?
CHARMIAN   O that brave Caesar!
CLEOPATRA
      Be choked with such another emphasis!
      Say "the brave Antony."
CHARMIAN   The valiant Caesar!
CLEOPATRA
70   By Isis, I will give thee bloody teeth
71   If thou with Caesar paragon again
      My man of men.

---

48 *arm-gaunt* toughened for war (?), battle-hungry (?)   **50** *dumbed* silenced
56 *make . . . his* imitate Antony's demeanor   **61** *posts* messengers   **62** *several*
distinct, separate   **71** *paragon* compare

CHARMIAN　　　　By your most gracious pardon,
I sing but after you.　　　　　　　　　　　　　　　　73
CLEOPATRA　　　　My salad days,
When I was green in judgment, cold in blood,
To say as I said then. But come, away,
Get me ink and paper.
He shall have every day a several greeting,
Or I'll unpeople Egypt.　　　　　　　　　　*Exeunt.*

*

∿ **II.1** *Enter Pompey, Menecrates, and Menas, in
warlike manner.*

POMPEY
If the great gods be just, they shall assist
The deeds of justest men.
MENECRATES　　　　　　Know, worthy Pompey,
That what they do delay, they not deny.
POMPEY
Whiles we are suitors to their throne, decays　　　4
The thing we sue for.
MENECRATES　　　　　　We, ignorant of ourselves,
Beg often our own harms, which the wise powers
Deny us for our good; so find we profit
By losing of our prayers.
POMPEY　　　　　　I shall do well:
The people love me, and the sea is mine;
My powers are crescent, and my auguring hope　　10
Says it will come to th' full. Mark Antony　　　11
In Egypt sits at dinner and will make
No wars without doors. Caesar gets money where　13
He loses hearts. Lepidus flatters both,

---

73 *salad days* green youth
　　II.1 Messina　4–5 *Whiles . . . for* i.e., the thing we pray for loses its worth
even while we pray　10 *crescent* increasing; *auguring* prophesying　11 *it . . .
full* i.e., my hope (for victory) will come about completely　13 *without doors*
outside, on the battlefield (rather than in bed with Cleopatra)

Of both is flattered; but he neither loves,
Nor either cares for him.

MENAS   Caesar and Lepidus
Are in the field; a mighty strength they carry.

POMPEY
Where have you this? 'Tis false.

MENAS   From Silvius, sir.

POMPEY
He dreams. I know they are in Rome together,
20 Looking for Antony. But all the charms of love,
21 Salt Cleopatra, soften thy waned lip!
Let witchcraft join with beauty, lust with both,
Tie up the libertine in a field of feasts,
Keep his brain fuming. Epicurean cooks
25 Sharpen with cloyless sauce his appetite,
26 That sleep and feeding may prorogue his honor
27 Even till a Lethe'd dullness –
    Enter Varrius.   How now, Varrius?

VARRIUS
This is most certain that I shall deliver:
Mark Antony is every hour in Rome
30 Expected. Since he went from Egypt 'tis
31 A space for farther travel.

POMPEY   I could have given less matter
A better ear. Menas, I did not think
33 This amorous surfeiter would have donned his helm
For such a petty war. His soldiership
Is twice the other twain. But let us rear
36 The higher our opinion, that our stirring
Can from the lap of Egypt's widow pluck
38 The ne'er-lust-wearied Antony.

MENAS   I cannot hope
39 Caesar and Antony shall well greet together.

---

21 *Salt* lustful; *waned* faded 25 *cloyless* which never cloys 26 *prorogue* suspend 27 *Lethe'd dullness* i.e., an oblivion as deep as that which comes from drinking of the river Lethe in the underworld 31 *A space . . . travel* time enough for even a longer journey 33 *surfeiter* one who indulges to excess 36 *opinion* i.e., of ourselves 38 *hope* expect 39 *greet* get on

His wife that's dead did trespasses to Caesar;   40
His brother warred upon him, although I think   41
Not moved by Antony.
POMPEY   I know not, Menas,
How lesser enmities may give way to greater.
Were't not that we stand up against them all,
'Twere pregnant they should square between themselves,   45
For they have entertainèd cause enough
To draw their swords; but how the fear of us
May cement their divisions and bind up
The petty difference, we yet not know.
Be't as our gods will have't! It only stands   50
Our lives upon to use our strongest hands.
Come, Menas.   *Exeunt.*

*

∾ **II.2** *Enter Enobarbus and Lepidus.*

LEPIDUS
Good Enobarbus, 'tis a worthy deed,
And shall become you well, to entreat your captain
To soft and gentle speech.
ENOBARBUS   I shall entreat him
To answer like himself. If Caesar move him,   4
Let Antony look over Caesar's head
And speak as loud as Mars. By Jupiter,
Were I the wearer of Antonio's beard,
I would not shave't today!   8
LEPIDUS   'Tis not a time
For private stomaching.   9
ENOBARBUS   Every time
Serves for the matter that is then born in't.   10

---

41 *brother* (cf. I.2.87–93) 45 *pregnant* obvious; *square* quarrel **50–51**
stands . . . upon is a matter of life and death
   II.2 Rome 4 *like himself* as befits his greatness 8 *I . . . shave't* i.e., I
would dare Caesar to pluck it (a gross insult) 9 *stomaching* resentment

LEPIDUS
But small to greater matters must give way.
ENOBARBUS
Not if the small come first.
LEPIDUS   Your speech is passion;
But pray you stir no embers up. Here comes
The noble Antony.
Enter Antony and Ventidius.
ENOBARBUS   And yonder, Caesar.
Enter Caesar, Maecenas, and Agrippa.
ANTONY
15   If we compose well here, to Parthia.
Hark, Ventidius.
CAESAR   I do not know,
Maecenas; ask Agrippa.
LEPIDUS
Noble friends,
That which combined us was most great, and let not
20   A leaner action rend us. What's amiss,
May it be gently heard. When we debate
Our trivial difference loud, we do commit
Murder in healing wounds. Then, noble partners,
24   The rather for I earnestly beseech,
Touch you the sourest points with sweetest terms,
26   Nor curstness grow to th' matter.
ANTONY   'Tis spoken well.
Were we before our armies, and to fight,
28   I should do thus.
Flourish.
CAESAR   Welcome to Rome.
30 ANTONY   Thank you.
CAESAR   Sit.
ANTONY   Sit, sir.

---

15 *compose* reach agreement **24** *The rather for* all the more because **26**
Nor . . . matter and let not ill temper make matters worse **28** *thus* (Antony
makes some courteous gesture)

CAESAR   Nay then.
    [They sit.]
ANTONY
  I learn you take things ill which are not so,
  Or being, concern you not.
CAESAR   I must be laughed at
  If, or for nothing or a little, I   36
  Should say myself offended, and with you
  Chiefly i' th' world; more laughed at that I should
  Once name you derogately, when to sound your name   39
  It not concerned me.   40
ANTONY
  My being in Egypt, Caesar, what was't to you?
CAESAR
  No more than my residing here at Rome
  Might be to you in Egypt; yet if you there
  Did practice on my state, your being in Egypt   44
  Might be my question.   45
ANTONY   How intend you, "practiced"?
CAESAR
  You may be pleased to catch at mine intent
  By what did here befall me. Your wife and brother
  Made wars upon me, and their contestation
  Was theme for you; you were the word of war.   49
ANTONY
  You do mistake your business: my brother never   50
  Did urge me in his act. I did inquire it   51
  And have my learning from some true reports   52
  That drew their swords with you. Did he not rather
  Discredit my authority with yours,
  And make the wars alike against my stomach,   55
  Having alike your cause? Of this my letters   56

---

36 *or . . . or* either . . . or   39 *derogately* disparagingly   44 *practice on* plot
against   45 *question* subject of debate   49 *you were . . . war* the war was carried on in your name   51 *urge me* use my name   52 *reports* reporters   55
stomach desire   56 *Having . . . cause* i.e., I have as much cause as you to resent it

57 Before did satisfy you. If you'll patch a quarrel,
    As matter whole you have to make it with,
    It must not be with this.

CAESAR   You praise yourself
60 By laying defects of judgment to me, but
    You patched up your excuses.

ANTONY   Not so, not so:
    I know you could not lack, I am certain on't,
    Very necessity of this thought, that I,
    Your partner in the cause 'gainst which he fought,
65 Could not with graceful eyes attend those wars
    Which fronted mine own peace. As for my wife,
    I would you had her spirit in such another;
68 The third o' th' world is yours, which with a snaffle
69 You may pace easy, but not such a wife.

70 ENOBARBUS   Would we had all such wives, that the men
    might go to wars with the women.

ANTONY
72 So much uncurbable, her garboils, Caesar,
    Made out of her impatience – which not wanted
    Shrewdness of policy too – I grieving grant
    Did you too much disquiet. For that you must
    But say I could not help it.

CAESAR   I wrote to you
    When rioting in Alexandria; you
    Did pocket up my letters, and with taunts
79 Did gibe my missive out of audience.

ANTONY   Sir,
80 He fell upon me, ere admitted, then;
81 Three kings I had newly feasted, and did want
    Of what I was i' th' morning; but next day
83 I told him of myself, which was as much
    As to have asked him pardon. Let this fellow

---

57 *patch* piece together 65 *with . . . attend* regard with pleasure 68 *snaffle*
bridle bit (to control a horse) 69 *pace* train to walk steadily (i.e., one third
of the world is an easily managed horse) 72 *garboils* commotions 79 *missive* messenger (see I.1.18 ff.) 81–82 *did . . . morning* was not myself 83
myself my condition

Be nothing of our strife: if we contend,
Out of our question wipe him.   86

CAESAR   You have broken
The article of your oath, which you shall never
Have tongue to charge me with.

LEPIDUS   Soft, Caesar.

ANTONY
No, Lepidus; let him speak.   90
The honor is sacred which he talks on now,
Supposing that I lacked it. But on, Caesar,
The article of my oath —

CAESAR
To lend me arms and aid when I required them,
The which you both denied.

ANTONY   Neglected rather:
And then when poisoned hours had bound me up
From mine own knowledge. As nearly as I may,   97
I'll play the penitent to you. But mine honesty
Shall not make poor my greatness, nor my power   99
Work without it. Truth is, that Fulvia,   100
To have me out of Egypt, made wars here,
For which myself, the ignorant motive, do
So far ask pardon as befits mine honor
To stoop in such a case.

LEPIDUS   'Tis noble spoken.

MAECENAS
If it might please you to enforce no further
The griefs between ye; to forget them quite
Were to remember that the present need
Speaks to atone you.   108

LEPIDUS   Worthily spoken, Maecenas.

ENOBARBUS   Or, if you borrow one another's love for the
instant, you may, when you hear no more words of   110
Pompey, return it again. You shall have time to wrangle
in when you have nothing else to do.

---

86 *question* argument   97 *mine own knowledge* awareness of my actions   **99**
make poor demean   **108** *atone* reconcile

ANTONY
    Thou art a soldier only. Speak no more.

ENOBARBUS   That truth should be silent I had almost
    forgot.

ANTONY

116   You wrong this presence, therefore speak no more.

117 ENOBARBUS   Go to, then; your considerate stone.

CAESAR
    I do not much dislike the matter, but
    The manner of his speech; for't cannot be

120   We shall remain in friendship, our conditions
    So differing in their acts. Yet if I knew
    What hoop should hold us staunch, from edge to edge
    O' th' world I would pursue it.

AGRIPPA   Give me leave, Caesar.

CAESAR   Speak, Agrippa.

AGRIPPA
    Thou hast a sister by the mother's side,
    Admired Octavia. Great Mark Antony
    Is now a widower.

CAESAR   Say not so, Agrippa:
    If Cleopatra heard you, your reproof

130   Were well deserved of rashness.

ANTONY
    I am not married, Caesar: let me hear
    Agrippa further speak.

AGRIPPA
    To hold you in perpetual amity,
    To make you brothers, and to knit your hearts
    With an unslipping knot, take Antony
    Octavia to his wife, whose beauty claims
    No worse a husband than the best of men,
    Whose virtue and whose general graces speak

---

116 *presence* company   117 *considerate* (1) respectful, (2) thoughtful   **130**
of rashness because of your rashness (in ignoring Antony's bond to Cleopatra)

That which none else can utter. By this marriage
All little jealousies, which now seem great,   140
And all great fears, which now import their dangers,
Would then be nothing. Truths would be tales,   142
Where now half-tales be truths. Her love to both
Would each to other, and all loves to both,
Draw after her. Pardon what I have spoke,
For 'tis a studied, not a present thought,
By duty ruminated.
ANTONY   Will Caesar speak?
CAESAR
Not till he hears how Antony is touched
With what is spoke already.
ANTONY
What power is in Agrippa,   150
If I would say, "Agrippa, be it so,"
To make this good?
CAESAR   The power of Caesar, and
His power unto Octavia.
ANTONY   May I never
To this good purpose, that so fairly shows,   154
Dream of impediment. Let me have thy hand   155
Further this act of grace, and from this hour
The heart of brothers govern in our loves
And sway our great designs.
CAESAR   There's my hand.
     [They clasp hands.]
A sister I bequeath you, whom no brother
Did ever love so dearly. Let her live   160
To join our kingdoms and our hearts; and never
Fly off our loves again.   162
LEPIDUS   Happily, amen.

---

140 *jealousies* suspicions, mistrusts   **142–43** *would be . . . be* would be taken for . . . are taken for   **154** *so fairly shows* look so hopeful   **155–56** *Let . . . act* i.e., give me your hand as pledge of this agreement   **162** *Fly off* break away (from this agreement)

ANTONY
    I did not think to draw my sword 'gainst Pompey,
164   For he hath laid strange courtesies and great
    Of late upon me. I must thank him only,
166   Lest my remembrance suffer ill report:
    At heel of that, defy him.
LEPIDUS   Time calls upon's.
168   Of us must Pompey presently be sought,
    Or else he seeks out us.
ANTONY   Where lies he?
CAESAR
170   About the Mount Misena.
ANTONY
    What is his strength by land?
CAESAR
    Great and increasing; but by sea
173   He is an absolute master.
ANTONY   So is the fame.
    Would we had spoke together! Haste we for it,
    Yet, ere we put ourselves in arms, dispatch we
    The business we have talked of.
CAESAR   With most gladness,
    And do invite you to my sister's view,
    Whither straight I'll lead you.
ANTONY   Let us, Lepidus,
    Not lack your company.
LEPIDUS   Noble Antony,
180   Not sickness should detain me.   *Flourish. [Exeunt.]*
                    Mane[n]t Enobarbus, Agrippa, Maecenas.
MAECENAS   Welcome from Egypt, sir.
182 **ENOBARBUS**   Half the heart of Caesar, worthy Maecenas!
    My honorable friend, Agrippa.
AGRIPPA   Good Enobarbus.

---

164 *strange* unusual   **166** *remembrance* readiness to acknowledge favors
168 *presently* at once   **170** *Misena* (an Italian port)   **173** *fame* report   **182**
Half i.e., sharing it with Agrippa

MAECENAS   We have cause to be glad that matters are so
well digested. You stayed well by't in Egypt.   186

ENOBARBUS   Ay, sir, we did sleep day out of countenance   187
and made the night light with drinking.

MAECENAS   Eight wild boars roasted whole at a breakfast,
and but twelve persons there. Is this true?   190

ENOBARBUS   This was but as a fly by an eagle: we had   191
much more monstrous matter of feast, which worthily
deserved noting.

MAECENAS   She's a most triumphant lady, if report be
square to her.   195

ENOBARBUS   When she first met Mark Antony, she pursed   196
up his heart, upon the river of Cydnus.

AGRIPPA   There she appeared indeed, or my reporter de-   198
vised well for her.

ENOBARBUS
I will tell you.   200
The barge she sat in, like a burnished throne,
Burned on the water. The poop was beaten gold;
Purple the sails, and so perfumèd that
The winds were lovesick with them. The oars were silver,
Which to the tune of flutes kept stroke and made
The water which they beat to follow faster,
As amorous of their strokes. For her own person,
It beggared all description. She did lie
In her pavilion, cloth-of-gold of tissue,   209
O'erpicturing that Venus where we see   210
The fancy outwork nature. On each side her   211
Stood pretty dimpled boys, like smiling Cupids,

---

186 *digested* arranged; *stayed . . . by't* kept at it, "lived it up"   **187–88** *we . . .
drinking* i.e., we ruffled the dignity of the day (personified) by sleeping
through it, and made night light (i.e., bright, lightheaded, and wanton) with
drinking parties   **191** *by* compared to   **195** *square* fair   **196–97** *pursed up*
pocketed, put in a purse (but with a suggestion of pursed lips for kissing)
198 *appeared* came before the public   **198–99** *devised* invented   **209** *cloth-
of-gold of tissue* cloth interwoven with gold threads   **210** *O'erpicturing* outdoing the picture of   **211** *fancy* i.e., the painter's imagination

ACT II.2

With divers-colored fans, whose wind did seem
214 To glow the delicate cheeks which they did cool,
And what they undid did.
AGRIPPA   O, rare for Antony.
ENOBARBUS
216 Her gentlewomen, like the Nereides,
217 So many mermaids, tended her i' th' eyes,
218 And made their bends adornings. At the helm
A seeming mermaid steers; the silken tackle
220 Swell with the touches of those flower-soft hands,
221 That yarely frame the office. From the barge
A strange invisible perfume hits the sense
Of the adjacent wharfs. The city cast
Her people out upon her; and Antony,
Enthroned i' th' marketplace, did sit alone,
226 Whistling to th' air; which, but for vacancy,
Had gone to gaze on Cleopatra too,
And made a gap in nature.
AGRIPPA   Rare Egyptian!
ENOBARBUS
Upon her landing, Antony sent to her,
230 Invited her to supper. She replied,
It should be better he became her guest,
Which she entreated. Our courteous Antony,
Whom ne'er the word of "no" woman heard speak,
Being barbered ten times o'er, goes to the feast,
235 And for his ordinary pays his heart
For what his eyes eat only.
AGRIPPA   Royal wench!
She made great Caesar lay his sword to bed;
238 He plowed her, and she cropped.

---

214 *glow* make glow (as if heated) 216 *Nereides* sea nymphs 217
tended . . . eyes waited on her every glance 218 *made . . . adornings* made
their postures of submission decorative (as in a tableau) 221 *yarely frame*
nimbly perform 226 *but for vacancy* except that it would have left a vacuum
235 *ordinary* meal 238 *cropped* bore fruit (i.e., Julius Caesar's son, Caesarion)

ENOBARBUS   I saw her once
   Hop forty paces through the public street;
   And having lost her breath, she spoke, and panted,   *240*
   That she did make defect perfection   *241*
   And, breathless, power breathe forth.

MAECENAS
   Now Antony must leave her utterly.

ENOBARBUS
   Never. He will not.
   Age cannot wither her, nor custom stale
   Her infinite variety. Other women cloy
   The appetites they feed, but she makes hungry
   Where most she satisfies. For vilest things
   Become themselves in her, that the holy priests   *249*
   Bless her when she is riggish.   *250*

MAECENAS
   If beauty, wisdom, modesty, can settle
   The heart of Antony, Octavia is
   A blessèd lottery to him.   *253*

AGRIPPA   Let us go.
   Good Enobarbus, make yourself my guest
   Whilst you abide here.

ENOBARBUS   Humbly, sir, I thank you. *Exeunt.*

*

∾ II.3 *Enter Antony, Caesar, Octavia between them.*

ANTONY
   The world and my great office will sometimes
   Divide me from your bosom.

OCTAVIA   All which time
   Before the gods my knee shall bow my prayers
   To them for you.

---

241 *defect* i.e., the resulting breathlessness   249 *Become . . . her* are so becoming to her   250 *riggish* lewd   253 *lottery* gift of fortune
   II.3 The house of Octavius Caesar

ANTONY   Good night, sir. My Octavia,
Read not my blemishes in the world's report:
6   I have not kept my square, but that to come
Shall all be done by th' rule. Good night, dear lady.
OCTAVIA   Good night, sir.
CAESAR   Good night.   *Exit [with Octavia].*
      Enter Soothsayer.
ANTONY
10   Now, sirrah: you do wish yourself in Egypt?
SOOTHSAYER
Would I had never come from thence, nor you thither.
ANTONY
If you can, your reason?
SOOTHSAYER
13   I see it in my motion, have it not in my tongue,
But yet hie you to Egypt again.
ANTONY   Say to me,
Whose fortunes shall rise higher, Caesar's or mine?
SOOTHSAYER
Caesar's.
Therefore, O Antony, stay not by his side.
18   Thy demon, that thy spirit which keeps thee, is
Noble, courageous, high, unmatchable,
20   Where Caesar's is not. But near him thy angel
21   Becomes afeard, as being o'erpowered. Therefore
Make space enough between you.
ANTONY   Speak this no more.
SOOTHSAYER
To none but thee; no more but when to thee.
If thou dost play with him at any game,
Thou art sure to lose; and of that natural luck
26   He beats thee 'gainst the odds. Thy luster thickens
When he shines by. I say again, thy spirit
Is all afraid to govern thee near him;
But he away, 'tis noble.

---

6 *square* carpenter's square (i.e., I have not followed the straight and narrow)
13 *motion* mind   18 *demon* guardian angel   21 *afeard* i.e., timorous   26
thickens dims

ANTONY   Get thee gone.
   Say to Ventidius I would speak with him.   30
                           Exit [Soothsayer.]
   He shall to Parthia. – Be it art or hap,   31
   He hath spoken true. The very dice obey him,
   And in our sports my better cunning faints   33
   Under his chance. If we draw lots, he speeds;   34
   His cocks do win the battle still of mine   35
   When it is all to naught, and his quails ever   36
   Beat mine, inhooped, at odds. I will to Egypt: 37
   And though I make this marriage for my peace,
   I' th' East my pleasure lies.
    Enter Ventidius.   O, come, Ventidius,
   You must to Parthia. Your commission's ready;
   Follow me and receive't.   *Exeunt.*   40

                             *

∾ **II.4** *Enter Lepidus, Maecenas, and Agrippa.*

LEPIDUS
   Trouble yourselves no further.
   Pray you, hasten your generals after.
AGRIPPA   Sir, Mark Antony
   Will e'en but kiss Octavia, and we'll follow.
LEPIDUS
   Till I shall see you in your soldier's dress,
   Which will become you both, farewell.
MAECENAS   We shall,
   As I conceive the journey, be at Mount   6
   Before you, Lepidus.
LEPIDUS   Your way is shorter;
   My purposes do draw me much about.   8
   You'll win two days upon me.

---

31 *art or hap* skill or chance **33** *cunning* skill **34** *chance* luck; *speeds* wins
35 *still* always **36** *it . . . naught* i.e., the odds are everything to nothing in
my favor **37** *inhooped* i.e., fighting confined within a hoop
   II.4 Lepidus's house **6** *Mount* i.e., Misena (see II.2.170) **8** *about*
roundabout

10   BOTH   Sir, good success.
      LEPIDUS   Farewell.   *Exeunt.*

                              *

∾ **II.5** *Enter Cleopatra, Charmian, Iras, and Alexas.*

CLEOPATRA
   Give me some music: music, moody food
   Of us that trade in love.
ALL   The music, ho!
      Enter Mardian the Eunuch.
CLEOPATRA
   Let it alone, let's to billiards. Come, Charmian.
CHARMIAN
   My arm is sore; best play with Mardian.
CLEOPATRA
   As well a woman with an eunuch played
   As with a woman. Come, you'll play with me, sir?
MARDIAN   As well as I can, madam.
CLEOPATRA
   And when good will is showed, though't come too short,
   The actor may plead pardon. I'll none now.
10   Give me mine angle, we'll to th' river: there,
   My music playing far off, I will betray
   Tawny-finned fishes. My bended hook shall pierce
   Their slimy jaws, and as I draw them up,
   I'll think them every one an Antony,
   And say, "Ah, ha! You're caught!"
CHARMIAN   'Twas merry when
   You wagered on your angling, when your diver
17   Did hang a salt fish on his hook, which he
   With fervency drew up.
CLEOPATRA   That time – O times! –
   I laughed him out of patience; and that night
20   I laughed him into patience; and next morn

_____
II.5 Alexandria   **10** *angle* fishing tackle   **17** *salt* dried

Ere the ninth hour I drunk him to his bed;
Then put my tires and mantles on him, whilst   22
I wore his sword Philippan.   23
    Enter a Messenger.   O, from Italy!
Ram thou thy fruitful tidings in mine ears,
That long time have been barren.

MESSENGER   Madam, madam –

CLEOPATRA
Antonio's dead! If thou say so, villain,
Thou kill'st thy mistress; but well and free,
If thou so yield him, there is gold, and here
My bluest veins to kiss, a hand that kings
Have lipped, and trembled kissing.   30

MESSENGER
First, madam, he is well.

CLEOPATRA
Why, there's more gold. But, sirrah, mark, we use
To say the dead are well; bring it to that,   33
The gold I give thee will I melt and pour
Down thy ill-uttering throat.

MESSENGER
Good madam, hear me.

CLEOPATRA   Well, go to, I will.
But there's no goodness in thy face if Antony   37
Be free and healthful; so tart a favor   38
To trumpet such good tidings! If not well,
Thou shouldst come like a Fury crowned with snakes,   40
Not like a formal man.   41

MESSENGER   Will't please you hear me?

CLEOPATRA
I have a mind to strike thee ere thou speak'st:
Yet, if thou say Antony lives, is well,

---

22 *tires* headdresses   23 *Philippan* (so called because he had beaten Brutus
and Cassius with it at the Battle of Philippi)   33 *well* i.e., in heaven;
bring . . . that say that you mean that   37 *goodness* i.e., truth   38 *tart a favor*
sour a face   41 *Not . . . man* not in human shape

Or friends with Caesar, or not captive to him,
I'll set thee in a shower of gold and hail
Rich pearls upon thee.

MESSENGER   Madam, he's well.

CLEOPATRA   Well said.

MESSENGER
And friends with Caesar.

CLEOPATRA   Thou'rt an honest man.

MESSENGER
Caesar and he are greater friends than ever.

CLEOPATRA
Make thee a fortune from me.

MESSENGER   But yet, madam –

CLEOPATRA
50   I do not like "But yet," it does allay
The good precedence: fie upon "But yet"!
"But yet" is a jailer to bring forth
Some monstrous malefactor. Prithee, friend,
Pour out the pack of matter to mine ear,
The good and bad together: he's friends with Caesar,
In state of health, thou say'st, and thou say'st, free.

MESSENGER
Free, madam? No. I made no such report,
He's bound unto Octavia.

CLEOPATRA   For what good turn?

MESSENGER
For the best turn i' th' bed.

CLEOPATRA   I am pale, Charmian.

MESSENGER
60   Madam, he's married to Octavia.

CLEOPATRA
The most infectious pestilence upon thee!
     Strikes him down.

MESSENGER
Good madam, patience.

CLEOPATRA   What say you?

50–51 *allay . . . precedence* debase what went before

> *Strikes him.*   Hence,
Horrible villain, or I'll spurn thine eyes   63
Like balls before me! I'll unhair thy head,   64
> *She hales him up and down.*
Thou shalt be whipped with wire and stewed in brine,
Smarting in ling'ring pickle.   66

MESSENGER   Gracious madam,
I that do bring the news made not the match.

CLEOPATRA
Say 'tis not so, a province I will give thee
And make thy fortunes proud. The blow thou hadst
Shall make thy peace for moving me to rage,   70
And I will boot thee with what gift beside   71
Thy modesty can beg.   72

MESSENGER   He's married, madam.

CLEOPATRA
Rogue, thou hast lived too long!
> *Draws a knife.*

MESSENGER   Nay, then I'll run.
What mean you, madam? I have made no fault.   *Exit.*

CHARMIAN
Good madam, keep yourself within yourself,
The man is innocent.

CLEOPATRA
Some innocents scape not the thunderbolt.
Melt Egypt into Nile, and kindly creatures
Turn all to serpents! Call the slave again.
Though I am mad, I will not bite him. Call!   80

CHARMIAN
He is afeard to come.

CLEOPATRA   I will not hurt him.
These hands do lack nobility, that they strike
A meaner than myself; since I myself

---

63 *spurn* kick   64 s.d. *hales* drags   66 *pickle* pickling solution   71 *boot* benefit   72 *modesty* humble condition

84   Have given myself the cause.
         Enter the Messenger again.
                                   Come hither, sir.
      Though it be honest, it is never good
      To bring bad news. Give to a gracious message
      An host of tongues, but let ill tidings tell
      Themselves when they be felt.
MESSENGER   I have done my duty.
CLEOPATRA
      Is he married?
90   I cannot hate thee worser than I do
      If thou again say "Yes."
MESSENGER   He's married, madam.
CLEOPATRA
92   The gods confound thee! Dost thou hold there still?
MESSENGER
      Should I lie, madam?
CLEOPATRA   O, I would thou didst,
94   So half my Egypt were submerged and made
      A cistern for scaled snakes! Go, get thee hence;
96   Hadst thou Narcissus in thy face, to me
      Thou wouldst appear most ugly. He is married?
MESSENGER
      I crave your highness' pardon.
CLEOPATRA   He is married?
MESSENGER
99   Take no offense that I would not offend you;
100   To punish me for what you make me do
101   Seems much unequal. He's married to Octavia.
CLEOPATRA
      O, that his fault should make a knave of thee,
103   That art not what thou'rt sure of! Get thee hence,

---

84 *cause* i.e., by loving Antony   92 *confound* destroy   94 *So* even though
96 *Hadst . . . face* were you as handsome as Narcissus (in Greek legend, Narcissus fell in love with his image reflected in a stream)   99 *Take . . . you* don't
be angry that I'd rather not anger you (i.e., by answering)   101 *unequal* un-
just   103 *That . . . of* i.e., who are not really hateful, like the news you bring

The merchandise which thou hast brought from Rome 104
Are all too dear for me. Lie they upon thy hand,
And be undone by 'em!   *[Exit Messenger.]*

CHARMIAN   Good your highness, patience.

CLEOPATRA
In praising Antony I have dispraised Caesar.

CHARMIAN   Many times, madam.

CLEOPATRA
I am paid for't now. Lead me from hence,
I faint. O Iras, Charmian! 'Tis no matter.   110
Go to the fellow, good Alexas. Bid him
Report the feature of Octavia, her years,
Her inclination; let him not leave out
The color of her hair. Bring me word quickly.

                              [Exit Alexas.]

Let him forever go! – let him not, Charmian,
Though he be painted one way like a Gorgon,   116
The other way's a Mars. *[To Mardian]* Bid you Alexas
Bring me word how tall she is. – Pity me, Charmian,
But do not speak to me. Lead me to my chamber.

                              Exeunt.

                    *

❧ **II.6** *Flourish. Enter Pompey [and Menas] at one door,*
     with Drum and Trumpet; at another, Caesar, Lepidus,
     Antony, Enobarbus, Maecenas, Agrippa, with Soldiers
     marching.

POMPEY
Your hostages I have, so have you mine;
And we shall talk before we fight.   2

CAESAR   Most meet
That first we come to words, and therefore have we

104–6 *merchandise . . . undone* (i.e., the salable goods, "merchandise," you
have brought – news of Antony's marriage – are too expensive, "dear," for
me to resell; they are yours to market and I hope you are bankrupted, "undone," when you seek a buyer) 116 *Gorgon* Medusa (the sight of whose
ugly face turned men to stone)
     II.6 Misenum 2 *meet* suitable

Our written purposes before us sent,
Which if thou hast considered, let us know
If 'twill tie up thy discontented sword
7   And carry back to Sicily much tall youth
That else must perish here.

POMPEY   To you all three,
The senators alone of this great world,
10   Chief factors for the gods: I do not know
11   Wherefore my father should revengers want,
Having a son and friends, since Julius Caesar,
13   Who at Philippi the good Brutus ghosted,
There saw you laboring for him. What was't
That moved pale Cassius to conspire? And what
Made all-honored, honest, Roman Brutus,
17   With the armed rest, courtiers of beauteous freedom,
To drench the Capitol, but that they would
Have one man but a man? And that is it
20   Hath made me rig my navy, at whose burden
The angered ocean foams, with which I meant
To scourge th' ingratitude that despiteful Rome
Cast on my noble father.

CAESAR   Take your time.

ANTONY
24   Thou canst not fear us, Pompey, with thy sails.
25   We'll speak with thee at sea. At land thou know'st
26   How much we do o'ercount thee.

POMPEY   At land indeed
27   Thou dost o'ercount me of my father's house:
28   But since the cuckoo builds not for himself,
29   Remain in't as thou mayst.

---

7 *tall* bold 10 *factors* agents, go-betweens 11 *Wherefore* why 13 *ghosted* haunted 17 *courtiers* wooers, followers 24 *fear* frighten 25 *speak* fight (see l. 3) 26 *o'ercount* outnumber 27 *o'ercount* cheat; *house* (Plutarch says that Antony had bought this house but not paid for it) 28 *cuckoo* (a bird that lays its eggs in the nests of other birds) 29 *as thou mayst* as long as you can

LEPIDUS　　　　　　　　　　Be pleased to tell us –
For this is from the present – how you take　　　　　30
The offers we have sent you.
CAESAR　　　　　　　　　　There's the point.
ANTONY
Which do not be entreated to, but weigh
What it is worth embraced.　　　　　　　　　33
CAESAR　　　　　　　　　　And what may follow,
To try a larger fortune.　　　　　　　　　　34
POMPEY　　　　　　　　You have made me offer
Of Sicily, Sardinia; and I must
Rid all the sea of pirates; then, to send
Measures of wheat to Rome. This 'greed upon,
To part with unhacked edges and bear back　　　38
Our targes undinted.　　　　　　　　　　39
CAESAR, ANTONY, LEPIDUS
　　　　　　　　　　That's our offer.
POMPEY　　　　　　　　　　　Know then
I came before you here a man prepared　　　　40
To take this offer; but Mark Antony
Put me to some impatience. Though I lose
The praise of it by telling, you must know,
When Caesar and your brother were at blows,
Your mother came to Sicily and did find
Her welcome friendly.
ANTONY　　　　　　　I have heard it, Pompey,
And am well studied for a liberal thanks,　　　47
Which I do owe you.
POMPEY　　　　　　Let me have your hand:
I did not think, sir, to have met you here.
ANTONY
The beds i' th' East are soft; and thanks to you,　50
That called me timelier than my purpose hither;
For I have gained by't.

---

30 *from the present* off the topic　**33** *embraced* if accepted　**34** *a larger fortune* i.e., war with the triumvirs　**38** *edges* swords　**39** *targes* shields　**47** *studied for* prepared with

CAESAR   Since I saw you last
  There's a change upon you.
POMPEY ·   Well, I know not
54 What counts harsh fortune casts upon my face,
  But in my bosom shall she never come
  To make my heart her vassal.
LEPIDUS   Well met here.
POMPEY
  I hope so, Lepidus. Thus we are agreed.
58 I crave our composition may be written,
  And sealed between us.
CAESAR   That's the next to do.
POMPEY
60 We'll feast each other ere we part, and let's
  Draw lots who shall begin.
ANTONY   That will I, Pompey.
POMPEY
  No, Antony, take the lot. But, first or last,
  Your fine Egyptian cookery shall have
  The fame. I have heard that Julius Caesar
  Grew fat with feasting there.
ANTONY   You have heard much.
POMPEY
  I have fair meanings, sir.
ANTONY   And fair words to them.
POMPEY
  Then so much have I heard,
  And I have heard Apollodorus carried –
ENOBARBUS
  No more of that. He did so.
POMPEY   What, I pray you?
ENOBARBUS
70 A certain queen to Caesar in a mattress.
POMPEY
  I know thee now. How far'st thou, soldier?

---

54 *counts* tallies (as on a scoring stick)   58 *composition* agreement

ENOBARBUS   Well;
  And well am like to do, for I perceive
  Four feasts are toward.   73
POMPEY   Let me shake thy hand,
  I never hated thee. I have seen thee fight
  When I have envied thy behavior.
ENOBARBUS   Sir,
  I never loved you much, but I ha' praised ye
  When you have well deserved ten times as much
  As I have said you did.   78
POMPEY   Enjoy thy plainness,
  It nothing ill becomes thee.
  Aboard my galley I invite you all: 80
  Will you lead, lords?
CAESAR, ANTONY, LEPIDUS   Show's the way, sir.
POMPEY   Come.
                        Exeunt [all but] Enobarbus and Menas.
MENAS   *[Aside]* Thy father, Pompey, would ne'er have
  made this treaty. – You and I have known, sir.   83
ENOBARBUS   At sea, I think.
MENAS   We have, sir.
ENOBARBUS   You have done well by water.
MENAS   And you by land.
ENOBARBUS   I will praise any man that will praise me,
  though it cannot be denied what I have done by land.
MENAS   Nor what I have done by water.   90
ENOBARBUS   Yes, something you can deny for your own
  safety: you have been a great thief by sea.
MENAS   And you by land.
ENOBARBUS   There I deny my land service. But give me
  your hand, Menas. If our eyes had authority, here they   95
  might take two thieves kissing.
MENAS   All men's faces are true, whatsome'er their hands
  are.

_____
73 *toward* coming up   78 *plainness* bluntness   83 *known* met   95 *authority*
i.e., the powers of arrest

99 ENOBARBUS   But there is never a fair woman has a true
100   face.

    MENAS   No slander, they steal hearts.

    ENOBARBUS   We came hither to fight with you.

    MENAS   For my part, I am sorry it is turned to a drink-
      ing. Pompey doth this day laugh away his fortune.

    ENOBARBUS   If he do, sure he cannot weep't back again.

106 MENAS   You've said, sir. We looked not for Mark Antony
      here. Pray you, is he married to Cleopatra?

    ENOBARBUS   Caesar's sister is called Octavia.

    MENAS   True, sir, she was the wife of Caius Marcellus.

110 ENOBARBUS   But she is now the wife of Marcus Anto-
      nius.

112 MENAS   Pray ye, sir?

    ENOBARBUS   'Tis true.

    MENAS   Then is Caesar and he forever knit together.

    ENOBARBUS   If I were bound to divine of this unity, I
      would not prophesy so.

117 MENAS   I think the policy of that purpose made more in
      the marriage than the love of the parties.

119 ENOBARBUS   I think so too. But you shall find the band
120   that seems to tie their friendship together will be the
      very strangler of their amity: Octavia is of a holy, cold,
122   and still conversation.

    MENAS   Who would not have his wife so?

    ENOBARBUS   Not he that himself is not so, which is Mark
      Antony. He will to his Egyptian dish again. Then shall
      the sighs of Octavia blow the fire up in Caesar, and, as
      I said before, that which is the strength of their amity
      shall prove the immediate author of their variance.
129   Antony will use his affection where it is. He married
130   but his occasion here.

---

99 *true* (1) honest, (2) without makeup   106 *You've said* i.e., you are quite
right   112 *Pray ye* i.e., how's that again   117 *made more* played more part
119 *band* bond, pledge   122 *still* quiet, gentle; *conversation* way of life   129
use . . . affection indulge his passion   130 *occasion* convenience

MENAS   And thus it may be. Come, sir, will you aboard?
I have a health for you.

ENOBARBUS   I shall take it, sir: we have used our throats
in Egypt.

MENAS Come, let's away.   *Exeunt.*

*

∾ **II.7** *Music plays. Enter two or three Servants, with a
banquet.*

FIRST SERVANT Here they'll be, man. Some o' their
plants are ill-rooted already; the least wind i' th' world   2
will blow them down.

SECOND SERVANT   Lepidus is high-colored.

FIRST SERVANT   They have made him drink alms drink.   5

SECOND SERVANT   As they pinch one another by the dis-
position, he cries out "No more," reconciles them to   7
his entreaty, and himself to th' drink.

FIRST SERVANT   But it raises the greater war between him
and his discretion.   10

SECOND SERVANT   Why, this it is to have a name in great
men's fellowship. I had as live have a reed that will do   12
me no service as a partisan I could not heave.   13

FIRST SERVANT   To be called into a huge sphere, and not   14
to be seen to move in't, are the holes where eyes should
be, which pitifully disaster the cheeks.   16

*A sennet sounded. Enter Caesar, Antony, Pompey,
Lepidus, Agrippa, Maecenas, Enobarbus, Menas, with
other Captains [and a Boy].*

II.7 Aboard Pompey's galley in the port of Misenum   **2** *plants* feet (with pun
on the usual sense: cf. *ill-rooted*)   **5** *alms drink* drink drunk on behalf of one
too far gone to continue his part in a round of toasts (Lepidus has been
tricked into drinking more than the rest)   **7** *No more* i.e., no more quarrel-
ing   **12** *live* lief   **13** *partisan* spear   **14–16** *To . . . cheeks* (Lepidus, a little
man in a part too big for him, is compared first to a heavenly body that fails
to perform its function in its *sphere,* and then to a face without eyes; *disaster,*
carrying the image back on itself, likens the face without eyes to a heaven
without stars.)   **16 s.d.** *sennet* distinctive set of trumpet notes announcing
important persons

ANTONY
    Thus do they, sir: they take the flow o' th' Nile
18   By certain scales i' th' pyramid. They know
19   By th' height, the lowness, or the mean, if dearth
20   Or foison follow. The higher Nilus swells,
    The more it promises; as it ebbs, the seedsman
    Upon the slime and ooze scatters his grain,
    And shortly comes to harvest.
LEPIDUS   You've strange serpents there.
ANTONY   Ay, Lepidus.
LEPIDUS   Your serpent of Egypt is bred now of your mud
    by the operation of your sun; so is your crocodile.
ANTONY   They are so.
POMPEY   Sit – and some wine! A health to Lepidus!
30 LEPIDUS   I am not so well as I should be, but I'll ne'er out.
31 ENOBARBUS   Not till you have slept. I fear me you'll be in
    till then.
LEPIDUS   Nay, certainly, I have heard the Ptolemies'
34   pyramises are very goodly things; without contradic-
    tion I have heard that.
MENAS
    Pompey, a word.
POMPEY   Say in mine ear. What is't?
MENAS
    Forsake thy seat, I do beseech thee, captain,
    And hear me speak a word.
POMPEY   Forbear me till anon.
    [Menas] whispers in's ear.
    This wine for Lepidus!
40 LEPIDUS   What manner o' thing is your crocodile?
ANTONY   It is shaped, sir, like itself, and it is as broad as
    it hath breadth; it is just so high as it is, and moves with

18 *scales* graduations   19–20 *dearth Or foison* famine or plenty   30 *ne'er out* never give up   31 *in* drunk   34 *pyramises* (apparently Lepidus's drunken rendering of "pyramids")

it own organs. It lives by that which nourisheth it, and　43
the elements once out of it, it transmigrates.　44

LEPIDUS　What color is it of?

ANTONY　Of it own color too.　46

LEPIDUS　'Tis a strange serpent.

ANTONY　'Tis so, and the tears of it are wet.　48

CAESAR　Will this description satisfy him?

ANTONY　With the health that Pompey gives him; else he　50
is a very epicure.

　　[Menas whispers again.]

POMPEY

　Go hang, sir, hang! Tell me of that? Away!
　Do as I bid you. – Where's this cup I called for?

MENAS

　If for the sake of merit thou wilt hear me,
　Rise from thy stool.

POMPEY　　　　　　　I think thou'rt mad.

　[Rises and walks aside.]　　　　　　The matter?

MENAS

　I have ever held my cap off to thy fortunes.　56

POMPEY

　Thou hast served me with much faith. What's else to
　　say? –
　Be jolly, lords.

ANTONY　　　　These quicksands, Lepidus,
　Keep off them, for you sink.

MENAS

　Wilt thou be lord of all the world?　60

POMPEY　　　　　　　　　　What say'st thou?

MENAS

　Wilt thou be lord of the whole world? That's twice.

POMPEY

　How should that be?

43, 46 *it own* its own　44 *transmigrates* i.e., its soul takes over the body of
some other creature (Antony is teasing the drunken Lepidus)　48 *tears* i.e.,
its "crocodile tears"　56 *held . . . off* i.e., been devoted

62 MENAS   But entertain it,
   And though thou think me poor, I am the man
   Will give thee all the world.
   POMPEY   Hast thou drunk well?
   MENAS
   No, Pompey, I have kept me from the cup.
   Thou art, if thou dar'st be, the earthly Jove:
67 Whate'er the ocean pales, or sky inclips,
   Is thine, if thou wilt ha't.
   POMPEY   Show me which way.
   MENAS
69 These three world-sharers, these competitors,
70 Are in thy vessel. Let me cut the cable;
   And when we are put off, fall to their throats.
   All there is thine.
   POMPEY   Ah, this thou shouldst have done,
   And not have spoke on't. In me 'tis villainy;
   In thee't had been good service. Thou must know
   'Tis not my profit that does lead mine honor;
76 Mine honor, it. Repent that e'er thy tongue
   Hath so betrayed thine act. Being done unknown,
   I should have found it afterwards well done,
   But must condemn it now. Desist, and drink.
   MENAS   [Aside]
80 For this, I'll never follow thy palled fortunes more.
   Who seeks, and will not take when once 'tis offered,
   Shall never find it more.
   POMPEY   This health to Lepidus!
   ANTONY
83 Bear him ashore. I'll pledge it for him, Pompey.
   ENOBARBUS
   Here's to thee, Menas.
   MENAS   Enobarbus, welcome.
   POMPEY   Fill till the cup be hid.

---

62 *But entertain it* only accept the idea   67 *pales* encircles   69 *competitors* partners   76 *Mine honor, it* i.e., my honor comes from profit   80 *palled* decayed   83 *I'll . . . him* (cf. l.5: Antony is now taking an alms drink)

ENOBARBUS   There's a strong fellow, Menas.
  [Points to the Servant who carries off Lepidus.]
MENAS   Why?
ENOBARBUS   A bears the third part of the world, man;   88
  seest not?
MENAS
  The third part then is drunk. Would it were all,   90
  That it might go on wheels!   91
ENOBARBUS
  Drink thou; increase the reels.   92
MENAS   Come.
POMPEY
  This is not yet an Alexandrian feast.
ANTONY
  It ripens towards it. Strike the vessels, ho!   95
  Here's to Caesar!   96
CAESAR   I could well forbear't.
  It's monstrous labor when I wash my brain
  And it grows fouler.
ANTONY   Be a child o' th' time.
CAESAR
  Possess it, I'll make answer;   99
  But I had rather fast from all four days   100
  Than drink so much in one.
ENOBARBUS   Ha, my brave emperor!
  Shall we dance now the Egyptian bacchanals
  And celebrate our drink?
POMPEY   Let's ha't, good soldier.
ANTONY
  Come, let's all take hands
  Till that the conquering wine hath steeped our sense
  In soft and delicate Lethe.   107
ENOBARBUS   All take hands.
  Make battery to our ears with the loud music;

___

88 *A* he   91 *go on wheels* whirl smoothly   92 *reels* whirls   95 *Strike the vessels* broach the casks   96 *forbear't* i.e., pass up this toast   99 *Possess it* down it   107 *Lethe* (cf. II.1.27 n.)

The while I'll place you; then the boy shall sing.
110   The holding every man shall bear as loud
As his strong sides can volley.
        Music plays. Enobarbus places them hand in hand.

                    The Song.

BOY *[Sings.]* Come, thou monarch of the vine,
113   Plumpy Bacchus with pink eyne!
                In thy vats our cares be drowned,
                With thy grapes our hairs be crowned.
                    Cup us till the world go round,
                    Cup us till the world go round!

CAESAR
    What would you more? Pompey, good night. Good
        brother,
119   Let me request you off. Our graver business
120   Frowns at this levity. Gentle lords, let's part;
    You see we have burned our cheeks. Strong Enobarb
    Is weaker than the wine, and mine own tongue
123   Splits what it speaks. The wild disguise hath almost
124   Anticked us all. What needs more words? Good night.
125   Good Antony, your hand.
POMPEY   I'll try you on the shore.
ANTONY
    And shall, sir. Give's your hand.
POMPEY   O Antony,
    You have my father's house. But what, we are friends!
    Come down into the boat.
ENOBARBUS   Take heed you fall not.
            [Exeunt all but Enobarbus and Menas.]
    Menas, I'll not on shore.
MENAS   No, to my cabin.

---

110 *holding* refrain   113 *pink* half-closed   119 *off* to come away   123 *disguise* dancing and drinking   124 *Anticked* made fools of   125 *try you* compete with you in drinking

These drums! these trumpets, flutes! what!   130
Let Neptune hear we bid a loud farewell
To these great fellows. Sound and be hanged, sound out!
Sound a flourish, with drums.

ENOBARBUS
Hoo! Says a. There's my cap.

MENAS
Hoo! Noble captain, come.   *Exeunt.*

*

∾ **III.1** *Enter Ventidius as it were in triumph, the dead*
body of Pacorus borne before him [with Silius and
other Romans].

VENTIDIUS
Now, darting Parthia, art thou struck, and now   1
Pleased fortune does of Marcus Crassus' death
Make me revenger. Bear the king's son's body
Before our army. Thy Pacorus, Orodes,   4
Pays this for Marcus Crassus.   5

SILIUS   Noble Ventidius,
Whilst yet with Parthian blood thy sword is warm,
The fugitive Parthians follow. Spur through Media,
Mesopotamia, and the shelters whither
The routed fly. So thy grand captain, Antony,
Shall set thee on triumphant chariots and   10
Put garlands on thy head.

VENTIDIUS   O Silius, Silius,
I have done enough. A lower place, note well,   12
May make too great an act. For learn this, Silius,
Better to leave undone than by our deed
Acquire too high a fame when him we serve's away.
Caesar and Antony have ever won

III.1 A battlefield in Syria   1 *darting Parthia* (Parthian warriors threw
darts – spears – at their enemies and then retreated, protected by a volley of
arrows – the feared "Parthian shot," where seeming retreat was really attack)
4 *Orodes* King of Parthia   5 *Marcus Crassus* member of the first triumvirate,
killed by the Parthians   12 *A lower place* an underling

More in their officer than person. Sossius,
One of my place in Syria, his lieutenant,
For quick accumulation of renown,
20   Which he achieved by th' minute, lost his favor.
Who does i' th' wars more than his captain can
Becomes his captain's captain; and ambition,
The soldier's virtue, rather makes choice of loss
Than gain which darkens him.
I could do more to do Antonius good,
26   But 'twould offend him. And in his offense
27   Should my performance perish.

SILIUS   Thou hast, Ventidius, that
Without the which a soldier and his sword
Grants scarce distinction. Thou wilt write to Antony?

VENTIDIUS
30   I'll humbly signify what in his name,
That magical word of war, we have effected;
How with his banners and his well-paid ranks
33   The ne'er-yet-beaten horse of Parthia
34   We have jaded out o' th' field.

SILIUS   Where is he now?

VENTIDIUS
He purposeth to Athens; whither, with what haste
The weight we must convey with's will permit,
We shall appear before him. – On, there, pass along.

                             Exeunt.

*

∾ **III.2** *Enter Agrippa at one door, Enobarbus at
another.*

AGRIPPA
1   What, are the brothers parted?

ENOBARBUS
They have dispatched with Pompey; he is gone;

---

26 *in his offense* in offending him   27 *that* i.e., discretion   33 *horse* cavalry
34 *jaded* driven weary
    III.2 Caesar's house in Rome   1 *parted* departed

The other three are sealing. Octavia weeps   3
To part from Rome; Caesar is sad, and Lepidus
Since Pompey's feast, as Menas says, is troubled
With the greensickness.   6
AGRIPPA   'Tis a noble Lepidus.
ENOBARBUS
A very fine one. O, how he loves Caesar!
AGRIPPA
Nay, but how dearly he adores Mark Antony!
ENOBARBUS
Caesar? Why, he's the Jupiter of men.
AGRIPPA
What's Antony? The god of Jupiter.   10
ENOBARBUS
Spake you of Caesar? How! the nonpareil!
AGRIPPA
O Antony! O thou Arabian bird!   12
ENOBARBUS
Would you praise Caesar, say "Caesar"; go no further.
AGRIPPA
Indeed he plied them both with excellent praises.
ENOBARBUS
But he loves Caesar best, yet he loves Antony:
Hoo! Hearts, tongues, figures, scribes, bards, poets,
    cannot
Think, speak, cast, write, sing, number – hoo! –
His love to Antony. But as for Caesar,
Kneel down, kneel down, and wonder.
AGRIPPA   Both he loves.
ENOBARBUS
They are his shards, and he their beetle.   20
    [Trumpet within.]   So –
This is to horse. Adieu, noble Agrippa.

---

3 *sealing* concluding agreements 6 *greensickness* iron-deficiency anemia (according to Elizabethan lore, lovesick adolescent girls suffered this condition, and Lepidus is likened to a girl in his relations to Caesar and Antony) 12 *Arabian bird* i.e., unique (like the mythical phoenix, of which only one was supposed to exist at a time) 20 *shards* wings

AGRIPPA
> Good fortune, worthy soldier, and farewell!
>> *Enter Caesar, Antony, Lepidus, and Octavia.*

ANTONY
> No further, sir.

CAESAR
> You take from me a great part of myself;
> Use me well in't. Sister, prove such a wife
26 As my thoughts make thee, and as my farthest band
> Shall pass on thy approof. Most noble Antony,
28 Let not the piece of virtue which is set
> Betwixt us as the cement of our love
30 To keep it builded be the ram to batter
> The fortress of it: for better might we
32 Have loved without this mean, if on both parts
> This be not cherished.

ANTONY   Make me not offended
> In your distrust.

CAESAR   I have said.

ANTONY   You shall not find,
35 Though you be therein curious, the least cause
> For what you seem to fear. So the gods keep you
> And make the hearts of Romans serve your ends!
> We will here part.

CAESAR
> Farewell, my dearest sister, fare thee well.
40 The elements be kind to thee, and make
> Thy spirits all of comfort. Fare thee well.

OCTAVIA
> My noble brother!

ANTONY
> The April's in her eyes; it is love's spring,
> And these the showers to bring it on. Be cheerful.

26–27 *As my thoughts . . . approof* such as I think you are and as you will confirm my most extreme oath   **28** *piece* paragon   **32** *mean* intermediary   **35** *curious* punctiliously exacting

OCTAVIA
   Sir, look well to my husband's house; and –
CAESAR   What,
   Octavia?
OCTAVIA   I'll tell you in your ear.
ANTONY
   Her tongue will not obey her heart, nor can
   Her heart inform her tongue – the swansdown feather   48
   That stands upon the swell at the full of tide,
   And neither way inclines.   50
ENOBARBUS
   Will Caesar weep?   51
AGRIPPA   He has a cloud in's face.
ENOBARBUS
   He were the worse for that were he a horse;   52
   So is he, being a man.
AGRIPPA   Why, Enobarbus,
   When Antony found Julius Caesar dead,
   He cried almost to roaring; and he wept
   When at Philippi he found Brutus slain.
ENOBARBUS
   That year indeed he was troubled with a rheum.   57
   What willingly he did confound he wailed,   58
   Believe't, till I wept too.
CAESAR   No, sweet Octavia,
   You shall hear from me still; the time shall not   60
   Outgo my thinking on you.
ANTONY   Come, sir, come,
   I'll wrestle with you in my strength of love:
   Look, here I have you *[Embracing Caesar]*; thus I let
   you go,

48–50 *the swansdown . . . inclines* i.e., her feelings for husband and brother
are evenly balanced 51–59 (Enobarbus and Agrippa talk aside) 52 *horse*
(horses with darker markings [*clouds*] on the face were thought to be infe-
rior) 57 *rheum* running at the eyes 58 *confound* defeat 60 *still* always
60–61 *the time . . . you* i.e., my thoughts of you will not be left behind (as in
a race) by time

And give you to the gods.
CAESAR   Adieu, be happy!
LEPIDUS
   Let all the number of the stars give light
   To thy fair way!
CAESAR   Farewell, farewell!
      Kisses Octavia.
ANTONY   Farewell!
                           Trumpets sound. Exeunt.

                              *

∿ **III.3** *Enter Cleopatra, Charmian, Iras, and Alexas.*

CLEOPATRA
   Where is the fellow?
ALEXAS   Half afeard to come.
CLEOPATRA
   Go to, go to.
      Enter the Messenger as before.
                     Come hither, sir.
ALEXAS   Good majesty,
3   Herod of Jewry dare not look upon you
   But when you are well pleased.
CLEOPATRA   That Herod's head
   I'll have; but how, when Antony is gone
   Through whom I might command it? Come thou near.
MESSENGER
   Most gracious majesty!
CLEOPATRA   Didst thou behold Octavia?
MESSENGER
   Ay, dread queen.
CLEOPATRA   Where?
MESSENGER   Madam, in Rome.
   I looked her in the face, and saw her led
10   Between her brother and Mark Antony.

___

III.3 Alexandria   3 *Herod* i.e., even Herod (traditionally represented as a
tyrant)

CLEOPATRA
  Is she as tall as me?
MESSENGER   She is not, madam.
CLEOPATRA
  Didst hear her speak? Is she shrill-tongued or low?
MESSENGER
  Madam, I heard her speak; she is low-voiced.
CLEOPATRA
  That's not so good. He cannot like her long.   14
CHARMIAN
  Like her? O Isis! 'tis impossible.
CLEOPATRA
  I think so, Charmian. Dull of tongue, and dwarfish.
  What majesty is in her gait? Remember,
  If e'er thou lookedst on majesty.
MESSENGER   She creeps:
  Her motion and her station are as one.   19
  She shows a body rather than a life,   20
  A statue than a breather.
CLEOPATRA   Is this certain?
MESSENGER
  Or I have no observance.
CHARMIAN   Three in Egypt
  Cannot make better note.
CLEOPATRA   He's very knowing,
  I do perceive't. There's nothing in her yet.
  The fellow has good judgment.
CHARMIAN   Excellent.
CLEOPATRA
  Guess at her years, I prithee.
MESSENGER   Madam,
  She was a widow –
CLEOPATRA   Widow? Charmian, hark.
MESSENGER
  And I do think she's thirty.

---

14 *good* i.e., as I am   19 *Her . . . one* even in motion she is still

CLEOPATRA
29   Bear'st thou her face in mind? Is't long or round?
MESSENGER
30   Round even to faultiness.
CLEOPATRA
  For the most part, too, they are foolish that are so.
  Her hair, what color?
MESSENGER
  Brown, madam; and her forehead
34   As low as she would wish it.
CLEOPATRA   There's gold for thee.
  Thou must not take my former sharpness ill.
  I will employ thee back again; I find thee
  Most fit for business. Go, make thee ready;
38   Our letters are prepared.   *[Exit Messenger.]*
CHARMIAN   A proper man.
CLEOPATRA
  Indeed he is so. I repent me much
40   That so I harried him. Why, methinks, by him,
41   This creature's no such thing.
CHARMIAN   Nothing, madam.
CLEOPATRA
  The man hath seen some majesty, and should know.
CHARMIAN
  Hath he seen majesty? Isis else defend,
  And serving you so long!
CLEOPATRA
  I have one thing more to ask him yet, good Charmian –
  But 'tis no matter, thou shalt bring him to me
  Where I will write. All may be well enough.
CHARMIAN
  I warrant you, madam.   *Exeunt.*

*

---

29 *long or round* (thought to be signs, respectively, of prudence and folly)
34 *As . . . it* i.e., so low she would wish it no lower   **38** *proper* attractive   **40**
harried mistreated   **41** *no such thing* nothing much

❧ **III.4** *Enter Antony and Octavia.*

ANTONY
   Nay, nay, Octavia, not only that –
   That were excusable, that and thousands more
   Of semblable import – but he hath waged   3
   New wars 'gainst Pompey; made his will, and read it   4
   To public ear;
   Spoke scantly of me. When perforce he could not
   But pay me terms of honor, cold and sickly
   He vented them, most narrow measure lent me;   8
   When the best hint was given him, he not took't,
   Or did it from his teeth.   10
OCTAVIA   O, my good lord,
   Believe not all, or if you must believe,
   Stomach not all. A more unhappy lady,   12
   If this division chance, ne'er stood between,
   Praying for both parts.
   The good gods will mock me presently   15
   When I shall pray "O, bless my lord and husband!"
   Undo that prayer by crying out as loud
   "O, bless my brother!" Husband win, win brother,
   Prays, and destroys the prayer; no midway
   'Twixt these extremes at all.   20
ANTONY   Gentle Octavia,
   Let your best love draw to that point which seeks
   Best to preserve it. If I lose mine honor,
   I lose myself; better I were not yours
   Than yours so branchless. But as you requested,   24
   Yourself shall go between's. The meantime, lady,
   I'll raise the preparation of a war   26

III.4 Athens   3 *semblable* like   4 *read it* (to show the public what benefactions they might expect from him)   8 *narrow measure* little credit   10 *from his teeth* grudgingly   12 *Stomach* resent   15 *presently* at once   24 *branchless* pruned (of my honors)   26 *war* armed force (?)

27 Shall stain your brother. Make your soonest haste;
28 So your desires are yours.
OCTAVIA   Thanks to my lord.
    The Jove of power make me, most weak, most weak,
30 Your reconciler! Wars 'twixt you twain would be
    As if the world should cleave, and that slain men
    Should solder up the rift.
ANTONY
    When it appears to you where this begins,
    Turn your displeasure that way, for our faults
    Can never be so equal that your love
    Can equally move with them. Provide your going;
    Choose your own company, and command what cost
    Your heart has mind to.   *Exeunt.*

                    *

∾ **III.5** *Enter Enobarbus and Eros.*

ENOBARBUS   How now, friend Eros?
EROS   There's strange news come, sir.
ENOBARBUS   What, man?
EROS   Caesar and Lepidus have made wars upon Pompey.
5 ENOBARBUS   This is old. What is the success?
EROS   Caesar, having made use of him in the wars 'gainst
7   Pompey, presently denied him rivality, would not let
    him partake in the glory of the action; and not resting
    here, accuses him of letters he had formerly wrote to
10 Pompey; upon his own appeal, seizes him; so the poor
11 third is up till death enlarge his confine.
ENOBARBUS
12 Then, world, thou hast a pair of chaps, no more;
    And throw between them all the food thou hast,
    They'll grind the one the other. Where's Antony?

---

27 *stain* eclipse   28 *So . . . yours* that way you'll gain what you wish (?)
    III.5 5 *success* outcome   7 *rivality* partnership   10 *appeal* accusation   11
up jailed   12 *chaps* jaws

EROS
 He's walking in the garden – thus – and spurns   15
 The rush that lies before him; cries "Fool Lepidus!" 16
 And threats the throat of that his officer   17
 That murdered Pompey.
ENOBARBUS   Our great navy's rigged.
EROS
 For Italy and Caesar. More, Domitius:
 My lord desires you presently. My news   20
 I might have told hereafter.
ENOBARBUS   'Twill be naught;
 But let it be. Bring me to Antony.
EROS   Come, sir. *Exeunt.*

*

∾ **III.6** *Enter Agrippa, Maecenas, and Caesar.*

CAESAR
 Contemning Rome, he has done all this and more 1
 In Alexandria. Here's the manner of 't:
 I' th' marketplace on a tribunal silvered,   3
 Cleopatra and himself in chairs of gold
 Were publicly enthroned; at the feet sat
 Caesarion, whom they call my father's son,   6
 And all the unlawful issue that their lust
 Since then hath made between them. Unto her
 He gave the stablishment of Egypt, made her 9
 Of lower Syria, Cyprus, Lydia,   10
 Absolute queen.
MAECENAS   This in the public eye?
CAESAR
 I' th' common showplace, where they exercise. 12

---

15 *thus* (Eros imitates Antony's angry walking)   16 *rush* reed (a floor cover-
ing)   17 *that his officer* that officer of his
 III.6 Caesar's house in Rome 1 *Contemning* scorning   3 *tribunal* dais   6
my father's (Octavius, though actually a grandnephew, had been adopted by
Julius Caesar)   9 *stablishment* rule   12 *showplace* theater, arena

His sons he there proclaimed the kings of kings:
Great Media, Parthia, and Armenia
He gave to Alexander; to Ptolemy he assigned
Syria, Cilicia, and Phoenicia. She
17 In th' habiliments of the goddess Isis
That day appeared, and oft before gave audience,
As 'tis reported, so.

MAECENAS   Let Rome be thus
20 Informed.

AGRIPPA   Who, queasy with his insolence
Already, will their good thoughts call from him.

CAESAR
The people know it, and have now received
His accusations.

AGRIPPA   Who does he accuse?

CAESAR
Caesar, and that having in Sicily
25 Sextus Pompeius spoiled, we had not rated him
26 His part o' th' isle. Then does he say he lent me
Some shipping unrestored. Lastly, he frets
That Lepidus of the triumvirate
Should be deposed; and, being, that we detain
30 All his revenue.

AGRIPPA   Sir, this should be answered.

CAESAR
'Tis done already, and the messenger gone.
I have told him Lepidus was grown too cruel,
That he his high authority abused
And did deserve his change. For what I have conquered,
I grant him part; but then in his Armenia,
And other of his conquered kingdoms, I
Demand the like.

MAECENAS   He'll never yield to that.

CAESAR
Nor must not then be yielded to in this.

---

17 *Isis* (cf. I.2.63 n.)   20 *queasy* nauseated   25 *spoiled* despoiled; *rated* allot-
ted   26 *isle* i.e., Sicily

Enter Octavia with her train.

OCTAVIA
Hail, Caesar, and my lord! Hail, most dear Caesar!

CAESAR
That ever I should call thee castaway!   40

OCTAVIA
You have not called me so, nor have you cause.

CAESAR
Why have you stolen upon us thus? You come not
Like Caesar's sister. The wife of Antony
Should have an army for an usher, and
The neighs of horse to tell of her approach
Long ere she did appear. The trees by th' way
Should have borne men, and expectation fainted,
Longing for what it had not. Nay, the dust
Should have ascended to the roof of heaven,
Raised by your populous troops. But you are come   50
A market maid to Rome, and have prevented
The ostentation of our love; which, left unshown,
Is often left unloved. We should have met you   53
By sea and land, supplying every stage
With an augmented greeting.

OCTAVIA   Good my lord,
To come thus was I not constrained, but did it
On my free will. My lord, Mark Antony,
Hearing that you prepared for war, acquainted
My grievèd ear withal; whereon I begged
His pardon for return.   60

CAESAR   Which soon he granted,
Being an abstract 'tween his lust and him.   61

OCTAVIA
Do not say so, my lord.

CAESAR   I have eyes upon him,
And his affairs come to me on the wind.
Where he is now?

OCTAVIA   My lord, in Athens.

---

53 *left unloved* thought not to exist   61 *abstract* shortcut

CAESAR
    No, my most wrongèd sister, Cleopatra
    Hath nodded him to her. He hath given his empire
    Up to a whore, who now are levying
    The kings o' th' earth for war. He hath assembled
    Bocchus, the king of Libya; Archelaus,
70   Of Cappadocia; Philadelphos, King
    Of Paphlagonia; the Thracian king, Adallas;
    King Manchus of Arabia; King of Pont;
    Herod of Jewry; Mithridates, King
    Of Comagene; Polemon and Amyntas,
    The kings of Mede and Lycaonia;
    With a more larger list of scepters.
OCTAVIA
    Ay me most wretched,
    That have my heart parted betwixt two friends
    That do afflict each other!
CAESAR   Welcome hither.
80   Your letters did withhold our breaking forth,
    Till we perceived both how you were wrong led
82   And we in negligent danger. Cheer your heart:
    Be you not troubled with the time, which drives
    O'er your content these strong necessities;
    But let determined things to destiny
    Hold unbewailed their way. Welcome to Rome,
    Nothing more dear to me. You are abused
88   Beyond the mark of thought: and the high gods,
89   To do you justice, makes his ministers
90   Of us and those that love you. Best of comfort,
    And ever welcome to us.
AGRIPPA   Welcome, lady.
MAECENAS
    Welcome, dear madam.
    Each heart in Rome does love and pity you.

---

82 *negligent danger* danger through negligence **88** *mark* reach **89** *makes his* make their; *ministers* agents

Only th' adulterous Antony, most large   94
In his abominations, turns you off
And gives his potent regiment to a trull   96
That noises it against us.   97

OCTAVIA   Is it so, sir?

CAESAR
Most certain. Sister, welcome. Pray you
Be ever known to patience. My dear'st sister!   *Exeunt.* 99

*

❦ **III.7** *Enter Cleopatra and Enobarbus.*

CLEOPATRA
I will be even with thee, doubt it not.

ENOBARBUS
But why, why, why?

CLEOPATRA
Thou hast forspoke my being in these wars,   3
And sayst it is not fit.

ENOBARBUS   Well, is it, is it?

CLEOPATRA
Is't not denounced against us? Why should not we 5
Be there in person?

ENOBARBUS
    [Aside]   Well, I could reply:
If we should serve with horse and mares together,
The horse were merely lost; the mares would bear 8
A soldier and his horse.

CLEOPATRA   What is't you say?

ENOBARBUS
Your presence needs must puzzle Antony;   10
Take from his heart, take from his brain, from's time

---

94 *large* uninhibited 96 *regiment* rule; *trull* whore 97 *noises it* clamors
99 *Be . . . patience* be always calm
    III.7 Antony's camp near Actium 3 *forspoke* opposed 5 *denounced* declared 8 *merely* entirely 10 *puzzle* paralyze

What should not then be spared. He is already
Traduced for levity; and 'tis said in Rome
That Photinus, an eunuch, and your maids
Manage this war.

CLEOPATRA   Sink Rome, and their tongues rot
16 That speak against us! A charge we bear i' th' war,
17 And as the president of my kingdom will
Appear there for a man. Speak not against it,
I will not stay behind.

    Enter Antony and Canidius.

ENOBARBUS   Nay, I have done.
20 Here comes the emperor.

ANTONY   Is it not strange, Canidius,
That from Tarentum and Brundusium
He could so quickly cut the Ionian sea
23 And take in Toryne? – You have heard on't, sweet?

CLEOPATRA
Celerity is never more admired
Than by the negligent.

ANTONY   A good rebuke,
Which might have well becomed the best of men
To taunt at slackness. Canidius, we
Will fight with him by sea.

CLEOPATRA   By sea; what else?

CANIDIUS
29 Why will my lord do so?

ANTONY   For that he dares us to't.

ENOBARBUS
30 So hath my lord dared him to single fight.

CANIDIUS
Ay, and to wage this battle at Pharsalia,
Where Caesar fought with Pompey. But these offers,
Which serve not for his vantage, he shakes off;
And so should you.

---

16 *charge* responsibility   **17** *president* ruler   **23** *take in* seize   **29** *For that* because

ENOBARBUS   Your ships are not well manned;
  Your mariners are muleters, reapers, people   35
  Ingrossed by swift impress. In Caesar's fleet   36
  Are those that often have 'gainst Pompey fought;
  Their ships are yare, yours, heavy. No disgrace   38
  Shall fall you for refusing him at sea,   39
  Being prepared for land.   40
ANTONY   By sea, by sea.
ENOBARBUS
  Most worthy sir, you therein throw away
  The absolute soldiership you have by land,
  Distract your army, which doth most consist   43
  Of war-marked footmen, leave unexecuted
  Your own renownèd knowledge, quite forgo
  The way which promises assurance, and
  Give up yourself merely to chance and hazard
  From firm security.
ANTONY   I'll fight at sea.
CLEOPATRA
  I have sixty sails, Caesar none better.
ANTONY
  Our overplus of shipping will we burn,   50
  And with the rest full-manned, from th' head of Actium
  Beat th' approaching Caesar. But if we fail,
  We then can do't at land.
        Enter a Messenger.   Thy business?
MESSENGER
  The news is true, my lord, he is descried;
  Caesar has taken Toryne.
ANTONY
  Can he be there in person? 'Tis impossible;
  Strange that his power should be. Canidius,   57
  Our nineteen legions thou shalt hold by land

---

35 *muleters* mule drivers (i.e., peasants)   **36** *Ingrossed* collected wholesale;
impress draft   **38** *yare* nimble   **39** *fall* befall   **43** *Distract* divide   **57** *power*
army

And our twelve thousand horse. We'll to our ship.
60   Away, my Thetis!
            Enter a Soldier.   How now, worthy soldier?
SOLDIER
     O noble emperor, do not fight by sea,
     Trust not to rotten planks. Do you misdoubt
     This sword and these my wounds? Let th' Egyptians
64   And the Phoenicians go a-ducking; we
     Have used to conquer standing on the earth
     And fighting foot to foot.
ANTONY   Well, well, away!
            Exit Antony [with] Cleopatra and Enobarbus.
SOLDIER
     By Hercules, I think I am i' th' right.
CANIDIUS
68   Soldier, thou art; but his whole action grows
     Not in the power on't. So our leader's led,
70   And we are women's men.
SOLDIER   You keep by land
     The legions and the horse whole, do you not?
CANIDIUS
     Marcus Octavius, Marcus Justeius,
     Publicola, and Caelius are for sea;
     But we keep whole by land. This speed of Caesar's
75   Carries beyond belief.
SOLDIER   While he was yet in Rome,
76   His power went out in such distractions as
77   Beguiled all spies.
CANIDIUS   Who's his lieutenant, hear you?
SOLDIER
     They say, one Taurus.
CANIDIUS   Well I know the man.
            Enter a Messenger.

_____

60 *Thetis* a sea goddess   60 s.d. *Soldier* (this speaker may be identical with
Scarus in III.10 and IV.7)   64 *a-ducking* (1) jumping in the sea, (2) singing
68–69 *action . . . on't* battle plan does not acknowledge his force's strength
75 *Carries . . . belief* travels (like an arrow)   76 *distractions* detachments   77
Beguiled deceived

MESSENGER
    The emperor calls Canidius.
CANIDIUS
    With news the time's in labor and throws forth   80
    Each minute some.   *Exeunt.*

                         *

✇ **III.8** *Enter Caesar [and Taurus], with his Army,*
    marching.

CAESAR Taurus!
TAURUS My lord?
CAESAR
    Strike not by land; keep whole. Provoke not battle
    Till we have done at sea. Do not exceed
    The prescript of this scroll. Our fortune lies
    Upon this jump.   *Exeunt.* 6

                         *

✇ **III.9** *Enter Antony and Enobarbus.*

ANTONY
    Set we our squadrons on yond side o' th' hill
    In eye of Caesar's battle; from which place   2
    We may the number of the ships behold,
    And so proceed accordingly.   *Exit [with Enobarbus].*

                         *

✇ **III.10** *Canidius marcheth with his land army one*
    way over the stage, and Taurus, the lieutenant of
    Caesar, the other way. After their going in is heard the
    noise of a sea fight. Alarum. Enter Enobarbus.

ENOBARBUS
    Naught, naught, all naught! I can behold no longer.   1

III.8 A battlefield near Actium   6 *jump* hazard farther than expected
  III.9 2 *battle* battle line (of ships)
  III.10 1 *Naught* ruined

2   Th' *Antoniad,* the Egyptian admiral,

3   With all their sixty, fly and turn the rudder:

     To see't mine eyes are blasted.

       Enter Scarus.

SCARUS   Gods and goddesses,

5   All the whole synod of them!

ENOBARBUS   What's thy passion?

SCARUS

6   The greater cantle of the world is lost

     With very ignorance; we have kissed away

     Kingdoms and provinces.

ENOBARBUS   How appears the fight?

SCARUS

9   On our side like the tokened pestilence

10   Where death is sure. Yon ribaudred nag of Egypt –

     Whom leprosy o'ertake! – i' th' midst o' th' fight,

     When vantage like a pair of twins appeared,

13   Both as the same, or rather ours the elder,

14   The breese upon her, like a cow in June,

     Hoists sails, and flies.

ENOBARBUS

     That I beheld.

     Mine eyes did sicken at the sight, and could not

18   Endure a further view.

SCARUS   She once being luffed,

     The noble ruin of her magic, Antony,

20   Claps on his sea wing, and, like a doting mallard,

     Leaving the fight in height, flies after her.

     I never saw an action of such shame;

     Experience, manhood, honor, ne'er before

     Did violate so itself.

ENOBARBUS   Alack, alack!

      Enter Canidius.

---

2 *admiral* flagship   3 *sixty* i.e., sixty Egyptian ships   5 *synod* assembly   6 *cantle* segment   9 *like . . . pestilence* like the plague when its certain symptoms have been seen   10 *ribaudred* foul, obscene (?)   13 *elder* i.e., superior   14 *breese* stinging fly (with pun on "breeze")   18 *luffed* headed into the wind to fly (?), disengaged (?)   20 *mallard* drake

CANIDIUS
    Our fortune on the sea is out of breath
    And sinks most lamentably. Had our general
    Been what he knew himself, it had gone well.   27
    O, he has given example for our flight
    Most grossly by his own.   29
ENOBARBUS   Ay, are you thereabouts?
    Why then, good night indeed.   30
CANIDIUS
    Toward Peloponnesus are they fled.
SCARUS
    'Tis easy to't; and there I will attend
    What further comes.
CANIDIUS   To Caesar will I render
    My legions and my horse; six kings already
    Show me the way of yielding.
ENOBARBUS   I'll yet follow
    The wounded chance of Antony, though my reason   36
    Sits in the wind against me.   *[Exeunt.]*   37

                              ✳

❧ **III.11** *Enter Antony with Attendants.*

ANTONY
    Hark, the land bids me tread no more upon't,
    It is ashamed to bear me. Friends, come hither.
    I am so lated in the world that I   3
    Have lost my way forever. I have a ship
    Laden with gold: take that, divide it. Fly,
    And make your peace with Caesar.
ALL   Fly? Not we.
ANTONY
    I have fled myself and have instructed cowards

---

27 *what . . . himself* (cf. I.1.57–59)   29 *are you thereabouts* i.e., is that where
your thoughts are   36 *chance* fortunes   37 *Sits . . . me* dissuades me (reason
rides the contrary wind of Antony's ill fortune)
    III.11 Alexandria   3 *so . . . world* i.e., like a traveler after nightfall

To run and show their shoulders. Friends, be gone.
I have myself resolved upon a course
10   Which has no need of you. Be gone.
My treasure's in the harbor. Take it! O,
12   I followed that I blush to look upon.
My very hairs do mutiny, for the white
Reprove the brown for rashness, and they them
For fear and doting. Friends, be gone. You shall
Have letters from me to some friends that will
17   Sweep your way for you. Pray you look not sad
18   Nor make replies of loathness; take the hint
19   Which my despair proclaims. Let that be left
20   Which leaves itself. To the seaside straightway!
I will possess you of that ship and treasure.
Leave me, I pray, a little: pray you now,
23   Nay, do so; for indeed I have lost command,
Therefore I pray you. I'll see you by and by.
        Sits down.
        Enter Cleopatra led by Charmian, [Iras,] and Eros.
EROS   Nay, gentle madam, to him, comfort him.
IRAS   Do, most dear queen.
CHARMIAN   Do? Why, what else?
CLEOPATRA   Let me sit down. O Juno!
29   ANTONY   No, no, no, no, no.
30   EROS   See you here, sir?
ANTONY   O fie, fie, fie!
CHARMIAN   Madam!
IRAS   Madam, O good empress!
EROS   Sir, sir!
ANTONY
35   Yes, my lord, yes. He at Philippi kept
His sword e'en like a dancer, while I struck

---

12 *that* what   17 *Sweep* i.e., with Caesar   18 *loathness* reluctance   19 *that*
i.e., himself   23–24 *I . . . pray you* i.e., I have lost the right to order you, so I
entreat you   29–50 (Antony carries on an imaginary conversation and does
not recognize the others' presence)   35–36 *kept . . . dancer* i.e., never drew
his sword

The lean and wrinkled Cassius; and 'twas I
That the mad Brutus ended. He alone
Dealt on lieutenantry, and no practice had   39
In the brave squares of war: yet now – no matter.   40
CLEOPATRA   Ah, stand by.
EROS   The queen, my lord, the queen.
IRAS
Go to him, madam, speak to him;
He is unqualitied with very shame.   44
CLEOPATRA
Well then, sustain me. O!
EROS
Most noble sir, arise. The queen approaches.
Her head's declined, and death will seize her, but   47
Your comfort makes the rescue.
ANTONY
I have offended reputation,
A most unnoble swerving.   50
EROS   Sir, the queen.
ANTONY
O, whither hast thou led me, Egypt? See
How I convey my shame out of thine eyes
By looking back what I have left behind   53
'Stroyed in dishonor.
CLEOPATRA   O my lord, my lord,
Forgive my fearful sails! I little thought
You would have followed.
ANTONY   Egypt, thou knew'st too well
My heart was to thy rudder tied by th' strings,
And thou shouldst tow me after. O'er my spirit
Thy full supremacy thou knew'st, and that
Thy beck might from the bidding of the gods   60
Command me.

---

39 *Dealt on lieutenantry* relied on subordinates   **40** *squares* bodies of troops
in square formations   **44** *unqualitied* not himself   **47** *but* unless   **53** *looking back* thinking on the past   **60** *beck* beckoning

CLEOPATRA   O, my pardon!
ANTONY   Now I must
62   To the young man send humble treaties, dodge
63   And palter in the shifts of lowness, who
      With half the bulk o' th' world played as I pleased,
      Making and marring fortunes. You did know
      How much you were my conqueror, and that
      My sword, made weak by my affection, would
      Obey it on all cause.
CLEOPATRA   Pardon, pardon!
ANTONY
69   Fall not a tear, I say: one of them rates
70   All that is won and lost. Give me a kiss;
71   Even this repays me. – We sent our schoolmaster.
72   Is a come back? – Love, I am full of lead. –
      Some wine, within there, and our viands! Fortune knows
      We scorn her most when most she offers blows.
                                              Exeunt.

                          *

∾ **III.12** *Enter Caesar, Agrippa, [Thidias, and]*
   Dolabella, with others.

CAESAR
   Let him appear that's come from Antony.
   Know you him?
DOLABELLA   Caesar, 'tis his schoolmaster –
   An argument that he is plucked, when hither
   He sends so poor a pinion of his wing,
   Which had superfluous kings for messengers
   Not many moons gone by.
      Enter Ambassador from Antony.
CAESAR   Approach and speak.

---

62 *treaties* proposals **63** *palter* equivocate; *shifts of lowness* deceits of the
powerless **69** *Fall* let fall; *rates* equals **71** *schoolmaster* i.e., his children's
tutor **72** *lead* i.e., heavy grief
   III.12 The camp of Octavius Caesar in Egypt

AMBASSADOR
    Such as I am, I come from Antony.
    I was of late as petty to his ends
    As is the morn dew on the myrtle leaf
    To his grand sea.   10
CAESAR   Be't so. Declare thine office.
AMBASSADOR
    Lord of his fortunes he salutes thee, and
    Requires to live in Egypt; which not granted,   12
    He lessons his requests, and to thee sues   13
    To let him breathe between the heavens and earth,   14
    A private man in Athens. This for him.
    Next, Cleopatra does confess thy greatness,
    Submits her to thy might, and of thee craves
    The circle of the Ptolemies for her heirs,   18
    Now hazarded to thy grace.   19
CAESAR   For Antony,
    I have no ears to his request. The queen   20
    Of audience nor desire shall fail, so she   21
    From Egypt drive her all-disgracèd friend
    Or take his life there. This if she perform,
    She shall not sue unheard. So to them both.
AMBASSADOR
    Fortune pursue thee!   25
CAESAR   Bring him through the bands.
                      [Exit Ambassador.]
    [To Thidias]
    To try thy eloquence now 'tis time. Dispatch.
    From Antony win Cleopatra. Promise,
    And in our name, what she requires; add more,
    From thine invention, offers. Women are not
    In their best fortunes strong, but want will perjure   30
    The ne'er-touched vestal. Try thy cunning, Thidias;

---

10 *sea* i.e., the ultimate source of dew **12** *Requires* requests **13** *lessons* disciplines **14** *breathe* i.e., go on living **18** *circle* crown **19** *hazarded . . . grace* gambled on your mercy **21** *audience* a hearing; *so* provided **25** *bands* troops

32 Make thine own edict for thy pains, which we
    Will answer as a law.
THIDIAS   Caesar, I go.
CAESAR
34 Observe how Antony becomes his flaw,
35 And what thou think'st his very action speaks
    In every power that moves.
THIDIAS   Caesar, I shall.   *Exeunt.*

*

∾ **III.13** *Enter Cleopatra, Enobarbus, Charmian, and
Iras.*

CLEOPATRA
    What shall we do, Enobarbus?
ENOBARBUS   Think, and die.
CLEOPATRA
    Is Antony or we in fault for this?
ENOBARBUS
3   Antony only, that would make his will
    Lord of his reason. What though you fled
5   From that great face of war, whose several ranges
    Frighted each other? Why should he follow?
    The itch of his affection should not then
8   Have nicked his captainship, at such a point,
    When half to half the world opposed, he being
10 The meréd question. 'Twas a shame no less
11 Than was his loss, to course your flying flags
    And leave his navy gazing.
CLEOPATRA   Prithee peace.
    Enter the Ambassador, with Antony.
ANTONY
    Is that his answer?

32 *Make ... edict* name your own price (as reward) 34 *becomes his flaw*
takes his fall (and see I.1.49–51) 35–36 *And ... moves* and what you think
his every move reveals
    III.13 Cleopatra's palace, Alexandria 3 *will* desire 5 *ranges* battle lines
8 *nicked* (1) cut, (2) cheated 10 *meréd question* sole matter at issue 11
course chase

AMBASSADOR
  Ay, my lord.
ANTONY
  The queen shall then have courtesy, so she
  Will yield us up.
AMBASSADOR   He says so.
ANTONY   Let her know't. –
  To the boy Caesar send this grizzled head,
  And he will fill thy wishes to the brim
  With principalities.
CLEOPATRA   That head, my lord?
ANTONY
  To him again! Tell him he wears the rose   20
  Of youth upon him; from which the world should note
  Something particular. His coin, ships, legions   22
  May be a coward's, whose ministers would prevail   23
  Under the service of a child as soon
  As i' th' command of Caesar. I dare him therefore
  To lay his gay caparisons apart   26
  And answer me declined, sword against sword,   27
  Ourselves alone. I'll write it. Follow me.
                    [Exeunt Antony and Ambassador.]
ENOBARBUS *[Aside]*
  Yes, like enough, high-battled Caesar will   29
  Unstate his happiness and be staged to th' show   30
  Against a sworder! I see men's judgments are   31
  A parcel of their fortunes, and things outward   32
  Do draw the inward quality after them   33
  To suffer all alike. That he should dream,   34
  Knowing all measures, the full Caesar will   35

---

22 *Something particular* i.e., some personal heroism   23 *ministers* agents
26 *caparisons* trappings – i.e., "coin, ships, legions" (the folio reads *comparisons*)   27 *declined* i.e., in years and status   29 *high-battled* possessing powerful troops   30 *Unstate* abdicate   30–31 *be . . . sworder* be exposed as a public spectacle in a gladiatorial duel   31 *sworder* gladiator   32 *A parcel* i.e., part and parcel   33 *quality* nature   34 *To . . . alike* so that both decline together   35 *Knowing all measures* being a good judge (of power and weakness)

Answer his emptiness! Caesar, thou hast subdued
His judgment too.
  Enter a Servant.
SERVANT   A messenger from Caesar.
CLEOPATRA
What, no more ceremony? See, my women,
Against the blown rose may they stop their nose
40   That kneeled unto the buds. – Admit him, sir.
            [Exit Servant.]

ENOBARBUS   *[Aside]*
41   Mine honesty and I begin to square.
The loyalty well held to fools does make
Our faith mere folly: yet he that can endure
To follow with allegiance a fallen lord
Does conquer him that did his master conquer
And earns a place i' th' story.
  Enter Thidias.
CLEOPATRA   Caesar's will?
THIDIAS
Hear it apart.
CLEOPATRA   None but friends: say boldly.
THIDIAS
48   So, haply, are they friends to Antony.
ENOBARBUS
He needs as many, sir, as Caesar has,
50   Or needs not us. If Caesar please, our master
Will leap to be his friend; for us, you know,
52   Whose he is we are, and that is Caesar's.
THIDIAS   So.
Thus then, thou most renowned, Caesar entreats
54   Not to consider in what case thou stand'st
Further than he is Caesar.

---

41 *square* quarrel   48 *haply* most likely   52 *Whose . . . are* i.e., we are friends
with Antony's friends   54–55 *Not . . . Caesar* i.e., not to think about your
situation beyond realizing that you have to do with (a generous conqueror
like) Caesar

CLEOPATRA   Go on: right royal.

THIDIAS

He knows that you embrace not Antony
As you did love, but as you feared him.

CLEOPATRA   O!

THIDIAS

The scars upon your honor therefore he
Does pity as constrainèd blemishes,
Not as deserved.   60

CLEOPATRA   He is a god and knows
What is most right. Mine honor was not yielded,
But conquered merely.

ENOBARBUS   *[Aside]*   To be sure of that,
I will ask Antony. Sir, sir, thou art so leaky
That we must leave thee to thy sinking, for
Thy dearest quit thee.   *Exit Enobarbus.*

THIDIAS   Shall I say to Caesar
What you require of him? For he partly begs   66
To be desired to give. It much would please him
That of his fortunes you should make a staff
To lean upon. But it would warm his spirits
To hear from me you had left Antony   70
And put yourself under his shroud,   71
The universal landlord.

CLEOPATRA   What's your name?

THIDIAS

My name is Thidias.

CLEOPATRA   Most kind messenger,
Say to great Caesar this in deputation: 74
I kiss his conquering hand; tell him I am prompt
To lay my crown at's feet, and there to kneel.
Tell him, from his all-obeying breath, I hear   77
The doom of Egypt.   78

---

66 *require* request   **71** *shroud* shelter   **74** *in deputation* i.e., through you as a
deputy   **77** *all-obeying* that all obey   **78** *doom* judgment, verdict

THIDIAS   'Tis your noblest course:
Wisdom and fortune combating together,
80   If that the former dare but what it can,
No chance may shake it. Give me grace to lay
82   My duty on your hand.
CLEOPATRA   Your Caesar's father oft,
When he hath mused of taking kingdoms in,
Bestowed his lips on that unworthy place,
As it rained kisses.
        Enter Antony and Enobarbus.
ANTONY   Favors? By Jove that thunders!
What art thou, fellow?
THIDIAS   One that but performs
The bidding of the fullest man and worthiest
To have command obeyed.
ENOBARBUS   *[Aside]*   You will be whipped.
ANTONY
89   Approach there! Ah, you kite! Now, gods and devils!
90   Authority melts from me. Of late, when I cried "Ho!"
91   Like boys unto a muss, kings would start forth,
And cry "Your will?" Have you no ears? I am
93   Antony yet.
        Enter a Servant.
                    Take hence this jack and whip him.
ENOBARBUS   *[Aside]*
'Tis better playing with a lion's whelp
Than with an old one dying.
ANTONY   Moon and stars!
Whip him. Were't twenty of the greatest tributaries
That do acknowledge Caesar, should I find them
So saucy with the hand of she here – what's her name
Since she was Cleopatra? Whip him, fellows,
100   Till like a boy you see him cringe his face
And whine aloud for mercy. Take him hence.

---

80 *If . . . can* if discretion confines itself to the possible   **82** *My duty* i.e., a
kiss   **89** *kite* bird of prey, scavenger (also slang for "whore")   **91** *muss* scram-
ble   **93** *jack* knave

THIDIAS
   Mark Antony –
ANTONY   Tug him away. Being whipped,
   Bring him again. This jack of Caesar's shall
   Bear us an errand to him.
                  Exeunt [Servants] with Thidias.
   You were half blasted ere I knew you. Ha!   105
   Have I my pillow left unpressed in Rome,
   Forborne the getting of a lawful race,
   And by a gem of women, to be abused   108
   By one that looks on feeders?   109
CLEOPATRA   Good my lord –
ANTONY
   You have been a boggler ever.   110
   But when we in our viciousness grow hard –
   O misery on't! – the wise god seel our eyes,   112
   In our own filth drop our clear judgments, make us
   Adore our errors, laugh at's while we strut
   To our confusion.
CLEOPATRA   O, is't come to this?
ANTONY
   I found you as a morsel cold upon
   Dead Caesar's trencher; nay, you were a fragment   117
   Of Gneius Pompey's, besides what hotter hours,
   Unregistered in vulgar fame, you have   119
   Luxuriously picked out. For I am sure,   120
   Though you can guess what temperance should be,
   You know not what it is.
CLEOPATRA   Wherefore is this?
ANTONY
   To let a fellow that will take rewards
   And say "God quit you!" be familiar with   124
   My playfellow, your hand, this kingly seal

---

105 *blasted* (1) withered, (2) cursed **108** *abused* betrayed **109** *feeders* me-
nials **110** *boggler* shifty one **112** *seel* sew up **117** *trencher* plate; *fragment*
leftover **119** *vulgar fame* common gossip **120** *Luxuriously* lustfully **124**
quit repay

126   And plighter of high hearts. O that I were
        Upon the hill of Basan to outroar
        The hornèd herd! For I have savage cause,
129   And to proclaim it civilly were like
130   A haltered neck which does the hangman thank
131   For being yare about him.
        Enter a Servant with Thidias.
                          Is he whipped?

SERVANT
132   Soundly, my lord.
        ANTONY   Cried he and begged a pardon?

SERVANT
    He did ask favor.

ANTONY
    If that thy father live, let him repent
    Thou wast not made his daughter; and be thou sorry
    To follow Caesar in his triumph, since
    Thou hast been whipped for following him. Henceforth
    The white hand of a lady fever thee;
    Shake thou to look on't. Get thee back to Caesar,
140   Tell him thy entertainment. Look thou say
    He makes me angry with him, for he seems
    Proud and disdainful, harping on what I am,
    Not what he knew I was. He makes me angry,
    And at this time most easy 'tis to do't,
    When my good stars that were my former guides
146   Have empty left their orbs and shot their fires
    Into th' abysm of hell. If he mislike
    My speech and what is done, tell him he has
149   Hipparchus, my enfranchèd bondman, whom
150   He may at pleasure whip, or hang, or torture,
    As he shall like, to quit me. Urge it thou.
    Hence with thy stripes, be gone!   *Exit Thidias.*

126–28 *O . . . herd* (Supposing he wears the cuckold's horns, Antony wishes
to withdraw among the roaring bulls of Bashan, biblical symbols of cruelty.)
129 *like* to act like   131 *yare* nimble   132 *a* he   140 *entertainment* recep-
tion (here)   146 *orbs* the spheres in which they turn   149 *Hipparchus* (who
had earlier revolted to Caesar); *enfranchèd* freed

CLEOPATRA
  Have you done yet?   153
ANTONY   Alack, our terrene moon
  Is now eclipsed, and it portends alone
  The fall of Antony.   155
CLEOPATRA   I must stay his time.
ANTONY
  To flatter Caesar, would you mingle eyes
  With one that ties his points?   157
CLEOPATRA   Not know me yet?
ANTONY
  Coldhearted toward me?
CLEOPATRA   Ah, dear, if I be so,
  From my cold heart let heaven engender hail,
  And poison it in the source, and the first stone   160
  Drop in my neck; as it determines, so   161
  Dissolve my life! The next Caesarion smite,
  Till by degrees the memory of my womb,   163
  Together with my brave Egyptians all,
  By the discandying of this pelleted storm,   165
  Lie graveless, till the flies and gnats of Nile
  Have buried them for prey!
ANTONY   I am satisfied.
  Caesar sits down in Alexandria, where
  I will oppose his fate. Our force by land
  Hath nobly held; our severed navy too   170
  Have knit again, and fleet, threat'ning most sealike.   171
  Where hast thou been, my heart? Dost thou hear, lady?   172
  If from the field I shall return once more
  To kiss these lips, I will appear in blood;   174
  I and my sword will earn our chronicle.   175
  There's hope in't yet.

---

153 *our . . . moon* i.e., Cleopatra, our terrestrial Isis or moon goddess 155
stay his time wait out his fury 157 *one . . . points* his valet 161 *determines*
melts 163 *the memory . . . womb* i.e., my offspring 165 *discandying* melt-
ing (as if it were hard candy) 171 *fleet* are afloat 172 *heart* courage 174
in blood (1) bloody, (2) with blood up, spirited 175 *our chronicle* our place
in history

CLEOPATRA
That's my brave lord!
ANTONY
I will be treble-sinewed, -hearted, -breathed,
179   And fight maliciously; for when mine hours
180   Were nice and lucky, men did ransom lives
Of me for jests; but now I'll set my teeth
And send to darkness all that stop me. Come,
183   Let's have one other gaudy night. Call to me
All my sad captains; fill our bowls once more;
Let's mock the midnight bell.
CLEOPATRA   It is my birthday.
I had thought t' have held it poor, but since my lord
Is Antony again, I will be Cleopatra.
ANTONY
We will yet do well.
CLEOPATRA
Call all his noble captains to my lord.
ANTONY
190   Do so, we'll speak to them, and tonight I'll force
The wine peep through their scars. Come on, my queen,
192   There's sap in't yet! The next time I do fight,
I'll make death love me, for I will contend
Even with his pestilent scythe.
                          Exeunt [all but Enobarbus].

ENOBARBUS
Now he'll outstare the lightning. To be furious
Is to be frighted out of fear, and in that mood
197   The dove will peck the estridge; and I see still
A diminution in our captain's brain
Restores his heart. When valor preys on reason,
It eats the sword it fights with. I will seek
Some way to leave him.   *Exit.*

                          *

---

179 *maliciously* fiercely   180 *nice* able to be "choosy"   183 *gaudy* luxurious
(i.e., in feasting and drinking)   192 *sap* i.e., life, hope   197 *estridge* hawk

◦ **IV.1** *Enter Caesar, Agrippa, and Maecenas, with his Army, Caesar reading a letter.*

CAESAR
He calls me boy, and chides as he had power
To beat me out of Egypt. My messenger
He hath whipped with rods; dares me to personal
    combat,
Caesar to Antony. Let the old ruffian know
I have many other ways to die, meantime
Laugh at his challenge.
MAECENAS   Caesar must think,
When one so great begins to rage, he's hunted
Even to falling. Give him no breath, but now
Make boot of his distraction. Never anger   9
Made good guard for itself.   10
CAESAR   Let our best heads
Know that tomorrow the last of many battles
We mean to fight. Within our files there are,   12
Of those that served Mark Antony but late,
Enough to fetch him in. See it done,   14
And feast the army; we have store to do't,
And they have earned the waste. Poor Antony! *Exeunt.* 16

                          ✳

◦ **IV.2** *Enter Antony, Cleopatra, Enobarbus, Charmian, Iras, Alexas, with others.*

ANTONY
He will not fight with me, Domitius?
ENOBARBUS   No.

IV.1 The camp of Octavius Caesar   9 *Make boot* take advantage   12 *files*
troops   14 *fetch him in* capture him   16 *waste* consumption (but not
"squandering")
    IV.2 Cleopatra's palace, Alexandria

ANTONY
  Why should he not?
ENOBARBUS
  He thinks, being twenty times of better fortune,
  He is twenty men to one.
ANTONY   Tomorrow, soldier,
5 By sea and land I'll fight. Or I will live,
  Or bathe my dying honor in the blood
7 Shall make it live again. Woo't thou fight well?
ENOBARBUS
8 I'll strike, and cry "Take all!"
ANTONY   Well said, come on;
  Call forth my household servants; let's tonight
10 Be bounteous at our meal.
      Enter three or four Servitors.
                            Give me thy hand,
  Thou hast been rightly honest, so hast thou,
  And thou, and thou, and thou. You have served me well,
13 And kings have been your fellows.
CLEOPATRA   What means this?
ENOBARBUS
  'Tis one of those odd tricks which sorrow shoots
  Out of the mind.
ANTONY   And thou art honest too.
16 I wish I could be made so many men,
  And all of you clapped up together in
  An Antony, that I might do you service
  So good as you have done.
ALL   The gods forbid!
ANTONY
20 Well, my good fellows, wait on me tonight;
  Scant not my cups, and make as much of me
  As when mine empire was your fellow too
  And suffered my command.

---

5 Or either   7 Woo't wilt (i.e., will thou)   8 Take all winner take all   13–15
(here and in ll. 23–24 Enobarbus and Cleopatra talk aside)   16 so many men
i.e., so many men as you are

CLEOPATRA   What does he mean?
ENOBARBUS
  To make his followers weep.
ANTONY   Tend me tonight;
  May be it is the period of your duty.   25
  Haply you shall not see me more; or if,
  A mangled shadow. Perchance tomorrow
  You'll serve another master. I look on you
  As one that takes his leave. Mine honest friends,
  I turn you not away, but like a master   30
  Married to your good service, stay till death.
  Tend me tonight two hours, I ask no more,
  And the gods yield you for't!   33
ENOBARBUS   What mean you, sir,
  To give them this discomfort? Look, they weep,
  And I, an ass, am onion-eyed. For shame!
  Transform us not to women.
ANTONY   Ho, ho, ho!
  Now the witch take me if I meant it thus!
  Grace grow where those drops fall! My hearty friends,   38
  You take me in too dolorous a sense,
  For I spake to you for your comfort, did desire you   40
  To burn this night with torches. Know, my hearts,
  I hope well of tomorrow and will lead you
  Where rather I'll expect victorious life
  Than death and honor. Let's to supper, come,
  And drown consideration.   *Exeunt.*

                          *

∾ **IV.3** *Enter a Company of Soldiers.*

FIRST SOLDIER
  Brother, good night. Tomorrow is the day.

---

25 *period* end   33 *yield* repay   38 *Grace grow* may virtues spring up (with a
pun on "grace" as one name for the herb rue)
   IV.3 Alexandria

SECOND SOLDIER
It will determine one way: fare you well.
Heard you of nothing strange about the streets?

FIRST SOLDIER
Nothing. What news?

SECOND SOLDIER
Belike 'tis but a rumor. Good night to you.

FIRST SOLDIER
Well, sir, good night.
They meet other Soldiers.

SECOND SOLDIER   Soldiers, have careful watch.

THIRD SOLDIER
And you. Good night, good night.
They place themselves in every corner of the stage.

FOURTH SOLDIER
8   Here we; and if tomorrow
Our navy thrive, I have an absolute hope
10   Our landmen will stand up.

THIRD SOLDIER   'Tis a brave army,
11   And full of purpose.
Music of the hautboys is under the stage.

SECOND SOLDIER   Peace! What noise?

FIRST SOLDIER   List, list!

SECOND SOLDIER
Hark!

FIRST SOLDIER   Music i' th' air.

THIRD SOLDIER   Under the earth.

FOURTH SOLDIER
13   It signs well, does it not?

THIRD SOLDIER   No.

FIRST SOLDIER   Peace, I say!
What should this mean?

---

8 *Here we* i.e., here is our post   11 s.d. *hautboys* loud-sounding musical in-
struments of the shawm family   13 *signs* signifies

SECOND SOLDIER
  'Tis the god Hercules, whom Antony loved,   15
  Now leaves him.
FIRST SOLDIER   Walk; let's see if other watchmen
  Do hear what we do.
SECOND SOLDIER   How now, masters?
ALL   *(Speak together.)*   How now?
  How now? Do you hear this?
FIRST SOLDIER   Ay. Is't not strange?
THIRD SOLDIER
  Do you hear, masters? do you hear?
FIRST SOLDIER
  Follow the noise so far as we have quarter.   20
  Let's see how it will give off.
ALL
  Content. 'Tis strange.   *Exeunt.*

                          *

❧ **IV.4** *Enter Antony and Cleopatra, with [Charmian and] others.*

ANTONY   Eros! Mine armor, Eros!
CLEOPATRA   Sleep a little.
ANTONY
  No, my chuck. Eros, come; mine armor, Eros.
    Enter Eros [with armor].
  Come, good fellow, put thine iron on.   3
  If fortune be not ours today, it is
  Because we brave her. Come.   5
CLEOPATRA   Nay, I'll help too.
  What's this for?
ANTONY   Ah, let be, let be! Thou art
  The armorer of my heart. False, false; this, this.   7

---

15 *Hercules* (cf. I.3.84–85 n.)   **20** *as . . . quarter* as our watch extends
  IV.4 The palace of Cleopatra   **3** *thine iron* i.e., this armor of mine   **5**
brave defy   **7** *False* wrong

CLEOPATRA
    Sooth, la, I'll help. Thus it must be.

ANTONY   Well, well,
    We shall thrive now. Seest thou, my good fellow?
10   Go, put on thy defenses.

EROS   Briefly, sir.

CLEOPATRA
    Is not this buckled well?

ANTONY   Rarely, rarely.
    He that unbuckles this, till we do please
    To doff't for our repose, shall hear a storm.
    Thou fumblest, Eros, and my queen's a squire
15   More tight at this than thou. Dispatch. O love,
    That thou couldst see my wars today and knew'st
    The royal occupation, thou shouldst see
18   A workman in't.
       Enter an armed Soldier.
                Good morrow to thee, welcome.
19   Thou look'st like him that knows a warlike charge.
20   To business that we love we rise betime
    And go to't with delight.

SOLDIER   A thousand, sir,
22   Early though't be, have on their riveted trim,
23   And at the port expect you.
       Shout. Trumpets flourish. Enter Captains and Soldiers.

CAPTAIN
    The morn is fair. Good morrow, General.

ALL
25   Good morrow, General.

ANTONY   'Tis well blown, lads.
    This morning, like the spirit of a youth
    That means to be of note, begins betimes.
28   So, so. Come, give me that. This way. Well said.

---

10 *Briefly* in a moment   **15** *tight* adroit   **18** *workman* craftsman, expert   **19** *charge* duty   **20** *betime* early   **22** *riveted trim* armor (in Shakespeare's day, but not Antony's, armor was sometimes riveted on the warrior)   **23** *port* gate   **25** *blown* opened (i.e., the morning)   **28** *said* done (spoken to Cleopatra, who is adjusting his armor or handing him something)

Fare thee well, dame. Whate'er becomes of me,
This is a soldier's kiss. Rebukable   30
And worthy shameful check it were to stand   31
On more mechanic compliment. I'll leave thee   32
Now like a man of steel. You that will fight,
Follow me close. I'll bring you to't. Adieu.
        Exeunt [Antony, Eros, Captains, and Soldiers].
CHARMIAN
    Please you retire to your chamber?
CLEOPATRA   Lead me.
    He goes forth gallantly. That he and Caesar might
    Determine this great war in single fight!
    Then Antony – but now – well, on.   *Exeunt.*

                        *

❧ **IV.5** *Trumpets sound. Enter Antony and Eros [, a*
        Soldier meeting them].

SOLDIER
    The gods make this a happy day to Antony!   1
ANTONY
    Would thou and those thy scars had once prevailed
    To make me fight at land!
SOLDIER   Hadst thou done so,
    The kings that have revolted and the soldier
    That has this morning left thee would have still
    Followed thy heels.
ANTONY   Who's gone this morning?
SOLDIER   Who?
    One ever near thee. Call for Enobarbus,
    He shall not hear thee, or from Caesar's camp
    Say "I am none of thine."
ANTONY   What sayest thou?

---

31 *check* reproof   32 *mechanic* ceremonious (and therefore "vulgar, com-
monplace")
    IV.5 Alexandria   1, 3, 6, 9, 11 *speech prefix Soldier* (The folio assigns the
first three speeches to Eros, the last two to "Soldier"; some editors think
Scarus is the speaker here; cf. *thy scars* in l. 2.)

SOLDIER   Sir,
10   He is with Caesar.
EROS   Sir, his chests and treasure
     He has not with him.
ANTONY   Is he gone?
SOLDIER   Most certain.
ANTONY
     Go, Eros, send his treasure after. Do it.
     Detain no jot, I charge thee. Write to him –
14   I will subscribe – gentle adieus and greetings;
     Say that I wish he never find more cause
     To change a master. O, my fortunes have
     Corrupted honest men! Dispatch. – Enobarbus!

                                          Exeunt.

                        *

∾ **IV.6** *Flourish. Enter Agrippa, Caesar, with
     Enobarbus, and Dolabella.*

CAESAR
     Go forth, Agrippa, and begin the fight.
     Our will is Antony be took alive;
     Make it so known.
AGRIPPA
     Caesar, I shall.   *[Exit.]*
CAESAR
5   The time of universal peace is near.
6   Prove this a prosperous day, the three-nooked world
     Shall bear the olive freely.
          Enter a Messenger.
MESSENGER   Antony
     Is come into the field.

_____

14 *subscribe* sign
     IV.6 The camp of Octavius Caesar   5 *universal peace* worldwide Roman
domination (so-called *Pax Romana*)   6 *Prove* should this prove to be; *three-
nooked* three-cornered (e.g., Africa, Asia, Europe, or a world once ruled by
three men, the triumvirs)

CAESAR   Go charge Agrippa
  Plant those that have revolted in the van,   9
  That Antony may seem to spend his fury   10
  Upon himself.   *Exeunt [all but Enobarbus].* 11

ENOBARBUS
  Alexas did revolt and went to Jewry on   12
  Affairs of Antony; there did dissuade   13
  Great Herod to incline himself to Caesar
  And leave his master Antony. For this pains
  Caesar hath hanged him. Canidius and the rest
  That fell away have entertainment, but   17
  No honorable trust. I have done ill,
  Of which I do accuse myself so sorely
  That I will joy no more.   20

    Enter a Soldier of Caesar's.

SOLDIER   Enobarbus, Antony
  Hath after thee sent all thy treasure, with
  His bounty overplus. The messenger
  Came on my guard and at thy tent is now
  Unloading of his mules.

ENOBARBUS   I give it you.

SOLDIER
  Mock not, Enobarbus.
  I tell you true. Best you safed the bringer   26
  Out of the host; I must attend mine office
  Or would have done't myself. Your emperor
  Continues still a Jove.   *Exit.*

ENOBARBUS
  I am alone the villain of the earth   30
  And feel I am so most. O Antony,
  Thou mine of bounty, how wouldst thou have paid
  My better service when my turpitude
  Thou dost so crown with gold! This blows my heart.   34
  If swift thought break it not, a swifter mean

---

9 *van* front lines   11 *himself* i.e., his own former soldiers   12 *Jewry* Judea
13 *dissuade* i.e., from Antony   17 *entertainment* employment   26 *safed* gave
safe-conduct to   34 *blows* (1) makes swell (?), (2) strikes (?)

Shall outstrike thought; but thought will do't, I feel.
I fight against thee? No, I will go seek
Some ditch wherein to die: the foul'st best fits
My latter part of life.   *Exit.*

                              *

∾ **IV.7** *Alarum. Drums and Trumpets. Enter Agrippa*
   [and Soldiers].

AGRIPPA
    Retire! We have engaged ourselves too far.
2   Caesar himself has work, and our oppression
    Exceeds what we expected.   *Exit [with Soldiers].*
         Alarums. Enter Antony, and Scarus wounded.
SCARUS
    O my brave emperor, this is fought indeed!
    Had we done so at first, we had driven them home
6   With clouts about their heads.
ANTONY   Thou bleed'st apace.
SCARUS
    I had a wound here that was like a T,
8   But now 'tis made an H.
         [Sound retreat] far off.
ANTONY   They do retire.
SCARUS
9   We'll beat 'em into bench holes. I have yet
10 Room for six scotches more.
         Enter Eros.
EROS
    They are beaten, sir, and our advantage serves
12 For a fair victory.

────────
IV.7 A field near Alexandria   **2** *our oppression* the pressure on us   **6** *clouts*
bandages   **8** *H* (pun on "ache," which was pronounced "aitch")   **9** *bench*
holes privy holes   **10** *scotches* gashes

SCARUS   Let us score their backs
  And snatch 'em up as we take hares, behind:
  'Tis sport to maul a runner.   14

ANTONY   I will reward thee
  Once for thy sprightly comfort and tenfold
  For thy good valor. Come thee on.   16

SCARUS   I'll halt after.

                                              Exeunt.

                              *

∾ **IV.8** *Alarum. Enter Antony again in a march; Scarus,*
  with others.

ANTONY
  We have beat him to his camp. Run one before
  And let the queen know of our gests. Tomorrow,   2
  Before the sun shall see's, we'll spill the blood
  That has today escaped. I thank you all,
  For doughty-handed are you and have fought
  Not as you served the cause, but as't had been
  Each man's like mine. You have shown all Hectors.   7
  Enter the city, clip your wives, your friends,   8
  Tell them your feats, whilst they with joyful tears
  Wash the congealment from your wounds and kiss   10
  The honored gashes whole.
    Enter Cleopatra.
    [To Scarus]   Give me thy hand;
  To this great fairy I'll commend thy acts,   12
  Make her thanks bless thee. – O thou day o' th' world,   13
  Chain mine armed neck; leap thou, attire and all,
  Through proof of harness to my heart, and there   15
  Ride on the pants triumphing!   16

_____

12 *score* mark   14 *runner* a foe who runs away   16 *halt* limp
    IV.8 Before the gates of Alexandria   2 *gests* deeds   7 *shown* proved; *Hectors* i.e., imitators of doomed Troy's greatest hero   8 *clip* hug   12 *fairy* being with magical powers   13 *day* light   15 *proof of harness* i.e., impenetrable armor   16 *Ride . . . pants* i.e., as if his heart were a panting steed

CLEOPATRA   Lord of lords!

17   O infinite virtue, com'st thou smiling from

18   The world's great snare uncaught?

ANTONY   My nightingale,
   We have beat them to their beds. What, girl! Though
     gray

20   Do something mingle with our younger brown, yet
     ha' we
   A brain that nourishes our nerves, and can

22   Get goal for goal of youth. Behold this man:
   Commend unto his lips thy favoring hand. –
   Kiss it, my warrior. – He hath fought today
   As if a god in hate of mankind had
   Destroyed in such a shape.

CLEOPATRA   I'll give thee, friend,
   An armor all of gold; it was a king's.

ANTONY

28   He has deserved it, were it carbuncled

29   Like holy Phoebus' car. Give me thy hand.

30   Through Alexandria make a jolly march;

31   Bear our hacked targets like the men that owe them.
   Had our great palace the capacity
   To camp this host, we all would sup together
   And drink carouses to the next day's fate,
   Which promises royal peril. Trumpeters,
   With brazen din blast you the city's ear,
   Make mingle with our rattling tabourines,
   That heaven and earth may strike their sounds together,
   Applauding our approach.   *Exeunt.*

*

---

17 *virtue* valor   18 *snare* dangers in the world outside their embrace (ll. 14–
16)   22 *Get . . . of* hold our own with   28 *carbuncled* jeweled   29 *holy
Phoebus' car* the sun god's chariot   31 *targets* shields; *owe* own

∾ **IV.9** *Enter a Sentry and his Company [of Watchmen].*
Enobarbus follows.

SENTRY
    If we be not relieved within this hour,
    We must return to th' court of guard. The night
    Is shiny, and they say we shall embattle   3
    By th' second hour i' th' morn.
FIRST WATCHMAN   This last day was
    A shrewd one to's.   5
ENOBARBUS   O, bear me witness, night –
SECOND WATCHMAN
    What man is this?   6
FIRST WATCHMAN   Stand close and list him.
ENOBARBUS
    Be witness to me, O thou blessèd moon,
    When men revolted shall upon record   8
    Bear hateful memory, poor Enobarbus did
    Before thy face repent!   10
SENTRY   Enobarbus?
SECOND WATCHMAN   Peace!
    Hark further.
ENOBARBUS
    O sovereign mistress of true melancholy,
    The poisonous damp of night disponge upon me,   13
    That life, a very rebel to my will,
    May hang no longer on me. Throw my heart
    Against the flint and hardness of my fault,
    Which, being dried with grief, will break to powder,   17
    And finish all foul thoughts. O Antony,
    Nobler than my revolt is infamous,
    Forgive me in thine own particular,   20

IV.9 The camp of Octavius Caesar   3 *shiny* light; *embattle* prepare for battle
5 *shrewd* bitterly painful   6 *list* listen to   8–9 *When . . . memory* when trai-
tors go down in history shamed   13 *disponge* squeeze (as from a sponge)
17 *Which* (refers to *heart*); *dried* (sorrow was thought to dry up the blood)
20 *in . . . particular* i.e., yourself

21   But let the world rank me in register
22   A master-leaver and a fugitive.
       O Antony! O Antony!
       [Dies.]
FIRST WATCHMAN   Let's speak
       To him.
SENTRY   Let's hear him, for the things he speaks
       May concern Caesar.
SECOND WATCHMAN   Let's do so. But he sleeps.
SENTRY
26   Swoons rather, for so bad a prayer as his
       Was never yet for sleep.
FIRST WATCHMAN   Go we to him.
SECOND WATCHMAN
       Awake, sir, awake, speak to us.
FIRST WATCHMAN   Hear you, sir?
SENTRY
29   The hand of death hath raught him.
       Drums afar off.
30   Hark! The drums demurely wake the sleepers.
       Let us bear him to th' court of guard.
       He is of note. Our hour is fully out.
SECOND WATCHMAN
       Come on then. He may recover yet.
                     Exeunt [with the body].

                  *

∾ **IV.10** *Enter Antony and Scarus, with their Army.*

ANTONY
       Their preparation is today by sea;
       We please them not by land.
SCARUS   For both, my lord.

---

21 *in register* in its records   **22** *master-leaver* (1) runaway servant, (2) outstanding traitor   **26** *Swoons* faints   **29** *raught* reached   **30** *demurely* softly
    IV.10 A field near Alexandria

ANTONY

> I would they'd fight i' th' fire or i' th' air;   3
> We'd fight there too. But this it is, our foot   4
> Upon the hills adjoining to the city
> Shall stay with us – order for sea is given;
> They have put forth the haven –
> Where their appointment we may best discover   8
> And look on their endeavor.   *Exeunt.*

*

∾ **IV.11** *Enter Caesar and his Army.*

CAESAR

> But being charged, we will be still by land,   1
> Which, as I take't, we shall; for his best force
> Is forth to man his galleys. To the vales,
> And hold our best advantage.   *Exeunt.*

*

∾ **IV.12** *Enter Antony and Scarus.*

ANTONY

> Yet they are not joined. Where yond pine does stand
> I shall discover all. I'll bring thee word
> Straight how 'tis like to go.   *Exit.*
SCARUS   Swallows have built
> In Cleopatra's sails their nests. The augurers
> Say they know not, they cannot tell, look grimly,
> And dare not speak their knowledge. Antony
> Is valiant, and dejected, and by starts
> His fretted fortunes give him hope and fear   8
> Of what he has, and has not.

----

3 *fire . . . air* i.e., everywhere (with the two other elements, water and earth, *sea* and *land* in ll. 1–2)   4 *foot* infantry   8 *appointment* equipment (hence "preparation")

IV.11 1 *But being* unless we are
IV.12 8 *fretted* (1) worn, (2) varied, mixed

Alarum afar off, as at a sea fight.
Enter Antony.

ANTONY   All is lost!
10   This foul Egyptian hath betrayed me:
     My fleet hath yielded to the foe, and yonder
     They cast their caps up and carouse together
13   Like friends long lost. Triple-turned whore! 'Tis thou
     Hast sold me to this novice, and my heart
     Makes only wars on thee. Bid them all fly,
16   For when I am revenged upon my charm,
     I have done all. Bid them all fly, be gone. *[Exit Scarus.]*
     O sun, thy uprise shall I see no more.
     Fortune and Antony part here, even here
20   Do we shake hands. All come to this? The hearts
     That spanieled me at heels, to whom I gave
22   Their wishes, do discandy, melt their sweets
23   On blossoming Caesar; and this pine is barked
     That overtopped them all. Betrayed I am.
25   O this false soul of Egypt! This grave charm,
     Whose eye becked forth my wars, and called them
         home,
27   Whose bosom was my crownet, my chief end,
28   Like a right gypsy hath at fast and loose
29   Beguiled me to the very heart of loss.
30   What, Eros, Eros!
         Enter Cleopatra.
                              Ah, thou spell! Avaunt!

CLEOPATRA
     Why is my lord enraged against his love?

ANTONY
     Vanish, or I shall give thee thy deserving
33   And blemish Caesar's triumph. Let him take thee
     And hoist thee up to the shouting plebeians;

---

13 *Triple-turned* i.e., from Pompey, from Julius Caesar, and now from himself   16 *charm* magician, charmer   22 *discandy* melt   23 *barked* stripped   25 *grave* deadly   27 *my crownet . . . end* the crown and goal of my life   28 *right* true; *fast and loose* (a confidence game)   29 *Beguiled* cheated, enticed   30 *Avaunt* be gone   33 *triumph* triumphal procession (in Rome)

Follow his chariot, like the greatest spot
Of all thy sex! Most monsterlike be shown
For poor'st diminutives, for dolts, and let   37
Patient Octavia plow thy visage up
With her preparèd nails.   *Exit Cleopatra.*
                    'Tis well thou'rt gone,
If it be well to live; but better 'twere   40
Thou fell'st into my fury, for one death
Might have prevented many. Eros, ho!
The shirt of Nessus is upon me. Teach me,   43
Alcides, thou mine ancestor, thy rage.   44
Let me lodge Lichas on the horns o' th' moon
And with those hands that grasped the heaviest club
Subdue my worthiest self. The witch shall die.
To the young Roman boy she hath sold me, and I fall
Under this plot. She dies for't. Eros, ho!   *Exit.*

                    *

❧ **IV.13** *Enter Cleopatra, Charmian, Iras, Mardian.*

CLEOPATRA
Help me, my women! O, he's more mad
Than Telamon for his shield; the boar of Thessaly   2
Was never so embossed.   3
CHARMIAN   To th' monument!
There lock yourself, and send him word you are dead.
The soul and body rive not more in parting   5
Than greatness going off.

———

37 *diminutives* little people (i.e., the populace)   43 *Nessus* (Fatally wounded
by Hercules with a poisoned arrow, the centaur Nessus persuaded Hercules'
wife to give his bloodstained shirt to her husband, telling her it would assure
his love for her. The shirt so poisoned Hercules that in his agony he threw his
page Lichas, who had brought it, to the skies and set about destroying himself.)   44 *Alcides* Hercules

  IV.13 Cleopatra's palace   2 *Telamon* Ajax Telamon (who went mad when
Achilles' shield was given not to him but to his rival, Ulysses); *boar of Thessaly* (sent by Artemis to ravage Thessaly in punishment for omitted sacrifices)
3 *embossed* foaming at the mouth from exhaustion; *monument* tomb (which,
like other Egyptian rulers, Cleopatra had prepared in advance)   5 *rive* rend

CLEOPATRA   To th' monument!
    Mardian, go tell him I have slain myself.
    Say that the last I spoke was "Antony"
    And word it, prithee, piteously. Hence, Mardian,
10 And bring me how he takes my death. To th' monu-
        ment!   *Exeunt.*

                        *

∾ **IV.14** *Enter Antony and Eros.*

ANTONY
    Eros, thou yet behold'st me?
EROS   Ay, noble lord.
ANTONY
    Sometime we see a cloud that's dragonish,
    A vapor sometime like a bear or lion,
    A towered citadel, a pendant rock,
    A forkèd mountain, or blue promontory
    With trees upon't that nod unto the world
    And mock our eyes with air. Thou hast seen these signs;
8   They are black vesper's pageants.
EROS   Ay, my lord.
ANTONY
    That which is now a horse, even with a thought
10 The rack dislimns and makes it indistinct
    As water is in water.
EROS   It does, my lord.
ANTONY
    My good knave Eros, now thy captain is
    Even such a body. Here I am Antony,
    Yet cannot hold this visible shape, my knave.
15 I made these wars for Egypt, and the queen,
    Whose heart I thought I had, for she had mine,
    Which whilst it was mine had annexed unto't

IV.14 Near Cleopatra's palace   **8** *black vesper's pageants* i.e., shows (the sun-
set) put on by vesper (evening) and heralding the coming of night (and figuratively, death)   **10** *rack dislimns* cloud effaces   **15** *Egypt* i.e., Cleopatra

A million more, now lost – she, Eros, has
Packed cards with Caesar and false-played my glory   19
Unto an enemy's triumph.   20
Nay, weep not, gentle Eros, there is left us
Ourselves to end ourselves.
  Enter Mardian.   O, thy vile lady!
She has robbed me of my sword.   23

MARDIAN   No, Antony.
My mistress loved thee and her fortunes mingled
With thine entirely.

ANTONY   Hence, saucy eunuch, peace!
She hath betrayed me and shall die the death.

MARDIAN
Death of one person can be paid but once,
And that she has discharged. What thou wouldst do
Is done unto thy hand. The last she spake   29
Was "Antony, most noble Antony!"   30
Then in the midst a tearing groan did break
The name of Antony; it was divided
Between her heart and lips: she rendered life,   33
Thy name so buried in her.

ANTONY   Dead, then?
MARDIAN   Dead.
ANTONY
Unarm, Eros. The long day's task is done,
And we must sleep.
  [To Mardian] That thou depart'st hence safe
Does pay thy labor richly. Go.   *Exit Mardian.*
          Off, pluck off!
The sevenfold shield of Ajax cannot keep   38
The battery from my heart. O, cleave, my sides!   39
Heart, once be stronger than thy continent,   40

---

19 *Packed cards* made a deceitful arrangement   20 *triumph* (1) victory, (2)
trump   23 *sword* manhood and soldiership   29 *unto . . . hand* ready without your effort   33–34 *she rendered . . . in her* i.e., she returned to the living
world the part of you figuratively written on her heart   38 *sevenfold* having
seven thicknesses   39 *battery* battering (of grief)   40 *continent* i.e., that
which contains thee

Crack thy frail case! Apace, Eros, apace.
No more a soldier. Bruisèd pieces, go;
You have been nobly borne. – From me awhile.

Exit Eros.

I will o'ertake thee, Cleopatra, and
Weep for my pardon. So it must be, for now
46   All length is torture; since the torch is out,
Lie down and stray no farther. Now all labor
Mars what it does; yea, very force entangles
49   Itself with strength. Seal then, and all is done.
50   Eros! – I come, my queen. – Eros! – Stay for me.
51   Where souls do couch on flowers, we'll hand in hand,
52   And with our sprightly port make the ghosts gaze.
53   Dido and her Aeneas shall want troops,
54   And all the haunt be ours. – Come, Eros, Eros!

Enter Eros.

EROS
What would my lord?

ANTONY   Since Cleopatra died
I have lived in such dishonor that the gods
Detest my baseness. I, that with my sword
Quartered the world and o'er green Neptune's back
59   With ships made cities, condemn myself to lack
60   The courage of a woman – less noble mind
Than she which by her death our Caesar tells
"I am conqueror of myself." Thou art sworn, Eros,
63   That, when the exigent should come, which now
Is come indeed, when I should see behind me
65   Th' inevitable prosecution of
Disgrace and horror, that on my command
Thou then wouldst kill me. Do't. The time is come.

---

46 *length* i.e., of life   49 *Seal* bring all to a close (as in sealing a document or
will)   51 *Where . . . flowers* i.e., in the Egyptian fields (the happy afterlife in
Greek myth)   52 *port* behavior   53 *want troops* lack admirers because we
are faithful, whereas Aeneas abandoned Dido to fulfill his Roman destiny
54 *haunt* company, group (of ghosted dead)   59 *to lack* for lacking   63 *exigent* need   65 *prosecution* pursuit

Thou strik'st not me, 'tis Caesar thou defeat'st.
Put color in thy cheek.

EROS   The gods withhold me!
Shall I do that which all the Parthian darts,   70
Though enemy, lost aim and could not?

ANTONY   Eros,
Wouldst thou be windowed in great Rome and see   72
Thy master thus with pleached arms, bending down   73
His corrigible neck, his face subdued   74
To penetrative shame, whilst the wheeled seat   75
Of fortunate Caesar, drawn before him, branded
His baseness that ensued?   77

EROS   I would not see't.

ANTONY
Come, then: for with a wound I must be cured.
Draw thou thy honest sword, which thou hast worn
Most useful for thy country.   80

EROS   O sir, pardon me.

ANTONY
When I did make thee free, swor'st thou not then
To do this when I bade thee? Do it at once,
Or thy precedent services are all   83
But accidents unpurposed. Draw, and come.

EROS
Turn from me then that noble countenance
Wherein the worship of the whole world lies.

ANTONY
Lo thee!

EROS
My sword is drawn.

ANTONY   Then let it do at once
The thing why thou hast drawn it.

---

72 *windowed* i.e., watching from a window   73 *pleached* folded   74 *corrigi-*
ble submissive   75 *penetrative* penetrating; *wheeled seat* chariot   77 *His . . .*
ensued the baseness of him that followed   83 *precedent* former

EROS   My dear master,
90   My captain, and my emperor, let me say,
     Before I strike this bloody stroke, farewell.

ANTONY
     'Tis said, man, and farewell.

EROS
     Farewell, great chief. Shall I strike now?

ANTONY   Now, Eros.

EROS
     Why, there then! Thus I do escape the sorrow
     Of Antony's death.
          Kills himself.

ANTONY   Thrice-nobler than myself!
     Thou teachest me, O valiant Eros, what
     I should, and thou couldst not. My queen and Eros
98   Have by their brave instruction got upon me
     A nobleness in record. But I will be
100 A bridegroom in my death and run into't
     As to a lover's bed. Come then, and, Eros,
     Thy master dies thy scholar. To do thus
          [Falls on his sword.]
     I learned of thee. How, not dead? Not dead?
104 The guard, ho! O, dispatch me!
          Enter [Dercetus and] a [Company of the] Guard.

FIRST GUARD   What's the noise?

ANTONY
     I have done my work ill, friends. O, make an end
     Of what I have begun.

SECOND GUARD   The star is fall'n.

109 FIRST GUARD   And time is at his period.

110 ALL   Alas, and woe!

98–99 *got . . . record* beaten me to a noble man in history   **104 s.d.** *Dercetus*
(this name and spelling derive from the first speech prefix for this character
in the folio and from Shakespeare's historical source; editors have also
adopted "Decretas" and "Dercetas")   **109** *period* end

ANTONY   Let him that loves me strike me dead.

FIRST GUARD   Not I.

SECOND GUARD   Nor I.

THIRD GUARD   Nor anyone.

Exeunt [the Guards].

DERCETUS

Thy death and fortunes bid thy followers fly.

This sword but shown to Caesar with this tidings

Shall enter me with him.   117

Enter Diomedes.

DIOMEDES

Where's Antony?

DERCETUS   There, Diomed, there.

DIOMEDES   Lives he?

Wilt thou not answer, man?   *[Exit Dercetus.]*

ANTONY

Art thou there, Diomed? Draw thy sword, and give me   *120*

Sufficing strokes for death.

DIOMEDES   Most absolute lord,

My mistress Cleopatra sent me to thee.

ANTONY

When did she send thee?

DIOMEDES   Now, my lord.

ANTONY   Where is she?

DIOMEDES

Locked in her monument. She had a prophesying fear

Of what hath come to pass; for when she saw –

Which never shall be found – you did suspect

She had disposed with Caesar, and that your rage   127

Would not be purged, she sent you word she was dead;   128

But fearing since how it might work, hath sent

Me to proclaim the truth, and I am come,   *130*

I dread, too late.

_____

117 *enter* recommend   127 *disposed* made terms   128 *purged* expelled

ANTONY
   Too late, good Diomed. Call my guard, I prithee.
DIOMEDES
   What ho, the emperor's guard! the guard, what ho!
   Come, your lord calls!
      Enter four or five of the Guard of Antony.
ANTONY
   Bear me, good friends, where Cleopatra bides.
   'Tis the last service that I shall command you.
FIRST GUARD
   Woe, woe are we, sir, you may not live to wear
   All your true followers out.
ALL   Most heavy day!
ANTONY
   Nay, good my fellows, do not please sharp fate
140 To grace it with your sorrows. Bid that welcome
   Which comes to punish us, and we punish it,
   Seeming to bear it lightly. Take me up.
   I have led you oft; carry me now, good friends,
   And have my thanks for all.
      *Exeunt [Diomedes and the Guard], bearing Antony
      [and Eros].*

                    *

 ∾ **IV.15** *Enter Cleopatra and her Maids aloft, with
      Charmian and Iras.*

CLEOPATRA
   O Charmian, I will never go from hence.
CHARMIAN
   Be comforted, dear madam.
CLEOPATRA   No, I will not.
   All strange and terrible events are welcome,

_____
IV.15 Before the monument of Cleopatra **s.d.** *Maids* (probably a redundant
reference to Charmian and Iras); *aloft* (the original staging of this scene and
of V.2 is unknown)

But comforts we despise. Our size of sorrow,   4
Proportioned to our cause, must be as great
As that which makes it.
    Enter Diomed [below].

                      How now? Is he dead?

CLEOPATRA

His death's upon him, but not dead.
Look out o' th' other side your monument;
His guard have brought him thither.
    Enter [below,] Antony, and the Guard [bearing him].

CLEOPATRA

O sun,   10
Burn the great sphere thou mov'st in, darkling stand   11
The varying shore o' th' world! O Antony,
Antony, Antony! Help, Charmian, help, Iras, help:
Help, friends below, let's draw him hither.

ANTONY   Peace!

Not Caesar's valor hath o'erthrown Antony,
But Antony's hath triumphed on itself.

CLEOPATRA

So it should be, that none but Antony
Should conquer Antony, but woe 'tis so!

ANTONY

I am dying, Egypt, dying; only
I here importune death awhile, until   20
Of many thousand kisses the poor last
I lay upon thy lips.   22

CLEOPATRA   I dare not, dear –
Dear my lord, pardon – I dare not,
Lest I be taken. Not th' imperious show
Of the full-fortuned Caesar ever shall
Be brooched with me, if knife, drugs, serpents have   26
Edge, sting, or operation. I am safe.
Your wife Octavia, with her modest eyes

---

4 *we* (royal plural) 11 *darkling* in the dark 20 *importune* beg (i.e., to delay) 22 *dare not* i.e., dare not descend to Antony's side 26 *brooched* adorned

29 And still conclusion, shall acquire no honor
30 Demuring upon me. But come, come, Antony!
    Help me, my women – we must draw thee up –
    Assist, good friends.

ANTONY   O, quick, or I am gone.

CLEOPATRA
    Here's sport indeed! How heavy weighs my lord!
34 Our strength is all gone into heaviness;
    That makes the weight. Had I great Juno's power,
    The strong-winged Mercury should fetch thee up
    And set thee by Jove's side. Yet come a little,
    Wishers were ever fools. O, come, come, come.
        They heave Antony aloft to Cleopatra.
    And welcome, welcome! Die when thou hast lived,
40 Quicken with kissing. Had my lips that power,
    Thus would I wear them out.

ALL   A heavy sight!

ANTONY
    I am dying, Egypt, dying.
    Give me some wine, and let me speak a little.

CLEOPATRA
    No, let me speak, and let me rail so high
45 That the false huswife Fortune break her wheel,
    Provoked by my offense.

ANTONY   One word, sweet queen.
    Of Caesar seek your honor, with your safety. O!

CLEOPATRA
    They do not go together.

ANTONY   Gentle, hear me:
    None about Caesar trust but Proculeius.

CLEOPATRA
50 My resolution and my hands I'll trust,
    None about Caesar.

---

29 *still conclusion* wordless censure   **30** *Demuring* looking gravely or soberly
(see V.2.54–55)   **34** *heaviness* (with pun on "grief")   **40** *Quicken* come back
to life   **45** *huswife* housewife (the word demeans a goddess and had a further
slang meaning of "worthless woman" – hence, "hussy")

ANTONY
　　The miserable change now at my end
　　Lament nor sorrow at, but please your thoughts
　　In feeding them with those my former fortunes,
　　Wherein I lived the greatest prince o' th' world,
　　The noblest: and do now not basely die,
　　Not cowardly put off my helmet to
　　My countryman. A Roman, by a Roman
　　Valiantly vanquished. Now my spirit is going,
　　I can no more.   60
CLEOPATRA   Noblest of men, woo't die?
　　Hast thou no care of me? Shall I abide
　　In this dull world, which in thy absence is
　　No better than a sty? O, see, my women,
　　　　[Antony dies.]
　　The crown o' th' earth doth melt. My lord!
　　O, withered is the garland of the war;   65
　　The soldier's pole is fallen. Young boys and girls   66
　　Are level now with men. The odds is gone,   67
　　And there is nothing left remarkable
　　Beneath the visiting moon.
　　　　[Starts to collapse.]
CHARMIAN   O, quietness, lady!   70
IRAS   She's dead too, our sovereign.
CHARMIAN   Lady!
IRAS   Madam!
CHARMIAN   O madam, madam, madam!
IRAS   Royal Egypt! Empress!
CHARMIAN   Peace, peace, Iras!
CLEOPATRA
　　No more but e'en a woman, and commanded
　　By such poor passion as the maid that milks
　　And does the meanest chares. It were for me   79

---

60 *woo't* wilt thou   **65** *garland . . . war* flower of all soldiers   **66** *pole* i.e.,
polestar (?) (other possible meanings include the maypole and the phallus)
67 *odds* measurement of great and little, significant and trivial   **79** *chares*
chores

80   To throw my scepter at the injurious gods,
      To tell them that this world did equal theirs
      Till they had stol'n our jewel. All's but naught.

83   Patience is sottish, and impatience does
      Become a dog that's mad. Then is it sin
      To rush into the secret house of death
      Ere death dare come to us? How do you, women?
      What, what! good cheer! Why, how now, Charmian?
      My noble girls! Ah, women, women, look!

89   Our lamp is spent, it's out! Good sirs, take heart.

90   We'll bury him; and then, what's brave, what's noble,
      Let's do't after the high Roman fashion,
      And make death proud to take us. Come, away.
      This case of that huge spirit now is cold.
      Ah, women, women! Come, we have no friend

95   But resolution and the briefest end.

                              Exeunt, bearing off Antony's body.
                         *

∾ **V.1** *Enter Caesar, Agrippa, Dolabella, Maecenas,*
      [Gallus, Proculeius,] with his Council of War.

CAESAR
      Go to him, Dolabella, bid him yield:

2   Being so frustrate, tell him he mocks

3   The pauses that he makes.

DOLABELLA   Caesar, I shall.   *[Exit.]*
      Enter Dercetus, with the sword of Antony.

CAESAR
      Wherefore is that? And what art thou that dar'st

5   Appear thus to us?

DERCETUS   I am called Dercetus.
      Mark Antony I served, who best was worthy

83–84 *Patience . . . mad* both patience and sorrow are now irrelevant to the
point   89 *sirs* i.e., Cleopatra's women   95 *briefest* quickest
      V.1 The camp of Octavius Caesar   2 *frustrate* helpless   2–3 *he mocks . . .
makes* i.e., to delay surrendering is ridiculous   3 s.d. *Dercetus* (see note
IV.14.104 s.d.)   5 *thus* i.e., with a naked, bloody sword

Best to be served. Whilst he stood up and spoke,
He was my master, and I wore my life
To spend upon his haters. If thou please
To take me to thee, as I was to him   *10*
I'll be to Caesar; if thou pleasest not,
I yield thee up my life.

CAESAR   What is't thou say'st?

DERCETUS
I say, O Caesar, Antony is dead.

CAESAR
The breaking of so great a thing should make
A greater crack. The round world
Should have shook lions into civil streets   *16*
And citizens to their dens. The death of Antony
Is not a single doom, in the name lay   *18*
A moiety of the world.   *19*

DERCETUS   He is dead, Caesar,
Not by a public minister of justice   *20*
Nor by a hirèd knife; but that self hand   *21*
Which writ his honor in the acts it did
Hath, with the courage which the heart did lend it,
Splitted the heart. This is his sword,
I robbed his wound of it. Behold it stained
With his most noble blood.

CAESAR   Look you sad, friends?
The gods rebuke me, but it is tidings
To wash the eyes of kings.

AGRIPPA   And strange it is
That nature must compel us to lament
Our most persisted deeds.   *30*

MAECENAS   His taints and honors
Waged equal with him.   *31*

---

16 *civil* city   18 *single doom* individual, particular fate (with allusion to
Doomsday, the Christian Last Judgment)   19 *moiety* half   21 *self* same   30
persisted i.e., persisted in   31 *Waged equal with* were evenly balanced in

AGRIPPA   A rarer spirit never
  Did steer humanity; but you gods will give us
  Some faults to make us men. Caesar is touched.

MAECENAS
  When such a spacious mirror's set before him,
  He needs must see himself.

CAESAR   O Antony,
  I have followed thee to this. But we do lance
  Diseases in our bodies. I must perforce
  Have shown to thee such a declining day
39 Or look on thine; we could not stall together
40 In the whole world. But yet let me lament
41 With tears as sovereign as the blood of hearts
42 That thou, my brother, my competitor
43 In top of all design, my mate in empire,
  Friend and companion in the front of war,
  The arm of mine own body, and the heart
46 Where mine his thoughts did kindle – that our stars,
47 Unreconciliable, should divide
  Our equalness to this. Hear me, good friends –
    Enter an Egyptian.
  But I will tell you at some meeter season.
50 The business of this man looks out of him;
  We'll hear him what he says. Whence are you?

EGYPTIAN
52 A poor Egyptian yet. The queen my mistress,
  Confined in all she has, her monument,
  Of thy intents desires instruction,
  That she preparedly may frame herself
  To th' way she's forced to.

CAESAR   Bid her have good heart.
  She soon shall know of us, by some of ours,

---

39 *stall* dwell   40–48 *But yet . . . to this* (this complex sentence begins as
praise of Antony, then restarts as a lament about fate)   41 *sovereign* potent
42 *competitor* partner   43 *In . . . design* in every lofty enterprise   46 *his* its
47 *Unreconciliable* (a rare spelling)   50 *looks . . . him* shows in his eyes   52
yet still (but only for a moment)

How honorable and how kindly we
Determine for her. For Caesar cannot live
To be ungentle.   60

EGYPTIAN   So the gods preserve thee!   *Exit.*

CAESAR
Come hither, Proculeius. Go and say
We purpose her no shame: give her what comforts
The quality of her passion shall require,   63
Lest, in her greatness, by some mortal stroke
She do defeat us, for her life in Rome
Would be eternal in our triumph. Go,   66
And with your speediest bring us what she says   67
And how you find of her.

PROCULEIUS   Caesar, I shall.   *Exit.*

CAESAR
Gallus, go you along. *[Exit Gallus.]* Where's Dolabella,
To second Proculeius?   70

ALL   Dolabella!

CAESAR
Let him alone, for I remember now
How he's employed. He shall in time be ready.
Go with me to my tent, where you shall see
How hardly I was drawn into this war,
How calm and gentle I proceeded still
In all my writings. Go with me, and see   76
What I can show in this.   *Exeunt.*

*

◌ **V.2** *Enter Cleopatra, Charmian, Iras.*

CLEOPATRA
My desolation does begin to make

---

63 *passion* grief 66 *eternal* eternally memorable 67 *with . . . speediest*
quick as you can 76 *writings* dispatches (to Antony)
  V.2 Before the monument of Cleopatra **s.d.** (the folio includes Mardian,
who has, however, no speech or action in the scene)

2 A better life. 'Tis paltry to be Caesar:
3 Not being Fortune, he's but Fortune's knave,
A minister of her will. And it is great
To do that thing that ends all other deeds,
Which shackles accidents and bolts up change;
7 Which sleeps, and never palates more the dung,
The beggar's nurse and Caesar's.
Enter Proculeius.

PROCULEIUS
Caesar sends greeting to the Queen of Egypt,
10 And bids thee study on what fair demands
Thou mean'st to have him grant thee.

CLEOPATRA   What's thy name?

PROCULEIUS
My name is Proculeius.

CLEOPATRA   Antony
Did tell me of you, bade me trust you, but
14 I do not greatly care to be deceived,
That have no use for trusting. If your master
Would have a queen his beggar, you must tell him
17 That majesty, to keep decorum, must
No less beg than a kingdom. If he please
To give me conquered Egypt for my son,
20 He gives me so much of mine own as I
Will kneel to him with thanks.

PROCULEIUS   Be of good cheer:
You're fallen into a princely hand. Fear nothing.
23 Make your full reference freely to my lord,
Who is so full of grace that it flows over
On all that need. Let me report to him
Your sweet dependency, and you shall find

---

2 *A better life* i.e., a truer estimate of values 3 *knave* servant 7 *palates* tastes; *dung* i.e., both the fruits of the earth and dirt, which are everyone's nurse (see I.1.35–36 for Antony's similar contempt) 14 *to be deceived* whether I am deceived or not 17 *keep decorum* i.e., act as majesty is expected to (in life and theater) 20 *as* that 23 *Make ... reference* entrust your case

A conqueror that will pray in aid for kindness   27
Where he for grace is kneeled to.

CLEOPATRA   Pray you, tell him
I am his fortune's vassal, and I send him
The greatness he has got. I hourly learn   30
A doctrine of obedience, and would gladly
Look him i' th' face.

PROCULEIUS   This I'll report, dear lady.
Have comfort, for I know your plight is pitied
Of him that caused it.
[Enter Roman Soldiers, who seize Cleopatra.]
You see how easily she may be surprised.
Guard her till Caesar come.

IRAS   Royal queen!

CHARMIAN   O Cleopatra! Thou art taken, queen.

CLEOPATRA
Quick, quick, good hands!
[Draws a dagger.]

PROCULEIUS   Hold, worthy lady, hold!
[Disarms her.]
Do not yourself such wrong, who are in this   40
Relieved, but not betrayed.   41

CLEOPATRA   What, of death too,
That rids our dogs of languish?   42

PROCULEIUS   Cleopatra,
Do not abuse my master's bounty by
Th' undoing of yourself. Let the world see
His nobleness well acted, which your death   45
Will never let come forth.

CLEOPATRA   Where art thou, death?
Come hither, come! Come, come, and take a queen
Worth many babes and beggars!

PROCULEIUS   O, temperance, lady!

---

27 *pray . . . kindness* ask your aid in naming kindnesses he can do for you
30 *got* i.e., won from me   41 *Relieved* rescued   42 *languish* frustrated longing   45 *acted* put into effect

CLEOPATRA
    Sir, I will eat no meat, I'll not drink, sir –
50   If idle talk will once be necessary –
51   I'll not sleep neither. This mortal house I'll ruin,
    Do Caesar what he can. Know, sir, that I
    Will not wait pinioned at your master's court
    Nor once be chastised with the sober eye
    Of dull Octavia. Shall they hoist me up
56   And show me to the shouting varletry
    Of censuring Rome? Rather a ditch in Egypt
    Be gentle grave unto me! Rather on Nilus' mud
    Lay me stark nak'd and let the water flies
60   Blow me into abhorring! Rather make
    My country's high pyramides my gibbet
    And hang me up in chains!
PROCULEIUS   You do extend
    These thoughts of horror further than you shall
    Find cause in Caesar.
       Enter Dolabella.
DOLABELLA   Proculeius,
    What thou hast done thy master Caesar knows,
    And he hath sent me for thee. For the queen,
    I'll take her to my guard.
PROCULEIUS   So, Dolabella,
    It shall content me best. Be gentle to her.
    [To Cleopatra]
    To Caesar I will speak what you shall please,
70   If you'll employ me to him.
CLEOPATRA   Say I would die.
        Exit Proculeius [with Soldiers].

DOLABELLA
    Most noble empress, you have heard of me?
CLEOPATRA
    I cannot tell.
DOLABELLA   Assuredly you know me.

---

50 *If . . . necessary* even if I must for the present moment resort to words, not acts   **51** *mortal house* body   **56** *varletry* mob   **60** *Blow me* make me swell

CLEOPATRA
  No matter, sir, what I have heard or known.
  You laugh when boys or women tell their dreams;
  Is't not your trick?
DOLABELLA   I understand not, madam.
CLEOPATRA
  I dreamt there was an emperor Antony.
  O, such another sleep, that I might see
  But such another man!
DOLABELLA   If it might please ye –
CLEOPATRA
  His face was as the heavens, and therein stuck   80
  A sun and moon, which kept their course and lighted
  The little O, th' earth.
DOLABELLA   Most sovereign creature –
CLEOPATRA
  His legs bestrid the ocean; his reared arm
  Crested the world; his voice was propertied   84
  As all the tunèd spheres, and that to friends;
  But when he meant to quail and shake the orb,   86
  He was as rattling thunder. For his bounty,
  There was no winter in't: an Antony it was   88
  That grew the more by reaping. His delights   89
  Were dolphinlike, they showed his back above   90
  The element they lived in. In his livery
  Walked crowns and crownets; realms and islands were   92
  As plates dropped from his pocket.   93
DOLABELLA   Cleopatra –
CLEOPATRA
  Think you there was or might be such a man
  As this I dreamt of?
DOLABELLA   Gentle madam, no.

84–85 *was propertied As* i.e., made music like **86** *quail* cow; *orb* earth **88**
Antony (the folio's reading, often emended to "autumn") **89** *grew . . . reaping* gave further gifts ("his bounty") where gifts had earlier been given **89–91** *His . . . lived in* i.e., his delight rose above ordinary pleasure-taking as a dolphin rises above its element, the sea **92** *crowns and crownets* i.e., kings and aristocrats **93** *plates* coins

CLEOPATRA
    You lie up to the hearing of the gods.
    But if there be nor ever were one such,
98 It's past the size of dreaming. Nature wants stuff
    To vie strange forms with fancy, yet t' imagine
100 An Antony were nature's piece 'gainst fancy,
    Condemning shadows quite.
DOLABELLA   Hear me, good madam.
    Your loss is as yourself, great; and you bear it
103 As answering to the weight. Would I might never
    O'ertake pursued success but I do feel,
    By the rebound of yours, a grief that smites
    My very heart at root.
CLEOPATRA   I thank you, sir.
    Know you what Caesar means to do with me?
DOLABELLA
    I am loath to tell you what I would you knew.
CLEOPATRA
    Nay, pray you, sir.
DOLABELLA   Though he be honorable –
CLEOPATRA
110 He'll lead me, then, in triumph?
DOLABELLA
    Madam, he will. I know't.
        Flourish. Enter Proculeius, Caesar, Gallus, Maecenas,
        and others of his train.

ALL
    Make way there! Caesar!
CAESAR
    Which is the Queen of Egypt?
DOLABELLA
    It is the emperor, madam.
        Cleopatra kneels.

_____

98–101 *Nature . . . quite* i.e., nature rarely can compete (as in a betting contest) with man's imagination in creating outstanding forms of excellence, but
if she created an Antony, he would be her masterpiece, outdoing the unreal
images of imagination altogether 103–4 *Would . . . do* i.e., may I never
have success if I do not

CAESAR
  Arise! You shall not kneel:
  I pray you rise, rise, Egypt.
CLEOPATRA   *[Rising]*   Sir, the gods
  Will have it thus. My master and my lord
  I must obey.
CAESAR   Take to you no hard thoughts.
  The record of what injuries you did us,
  Though written in our flesh, we shall remember   *120*
  As things but done by chance.
CLEOPATRA   Sole sir o' th' world,
  I cannot project mine own cause so well   *122*
  To make it clear, but do confess I have
  Been laden with like frailties which before
  Have often shamed our sex.
CAESAR   Cleopatra, know
  We will extenuate rather than enforce.   *126*
  If you apply yourself to our intents,   *127*
  Which towards you are most gentle, you shall find
  A benefit in this change; but if you seek
  To lay on me a cruelty by taking   *130*
  Antony's course, you shall bereave yourself
  Of my good purposes, and put your children
  To that destruction which I'll guard them from
  If thereon you rely. I'll take my leave.
CLEOPATRA
  And may, through all the world: 'tis yours, and we,
  Your scutcheons and your signs of conquest, shall   *136*
  Hang in what place you please. Here, my good lord.
    [Offering a scroll.]
CAESAR
  You shall advise me in all for Cleopatra.

---

122 *project* set forth   126 *enforce* emphasize (them)   127 *apply* conform
136 *scutcheons* coats of arms (here, those captured by the victor and tri-
umphantly displayed)

CLEOPATRA

139   This is the brief of money, plate, and jewels

140   I am possessed of. 'Tis exactly valued,
     Not petty things admitted. Where's Seleucus?
     [Enter Seleucus.]

SELEUCUS
     Here, madam.

CLEOPATRA
     This is my treasurer; let him speak, my lord,
     Upon his peril, that I have reserved
     To myself nothing. Speak the truth, Seleucus.

SELEUCUS

146   Madam, I had rather seel my lips
     Than to my peril speak that which is not.

CLEOPATRA   What have I kept back?

SELEUCUS
     Enough to purchase what you have made known.

CAESAR

150   Nay, blush not, Cleopatra. I approve
     Your wisdom in the deed.

CLEOPATRA   See, Caesar! O, behold,

152   How pomp is followed! Mine will now be yours,

153   And should we shift estates, yours would be mine.
     The ingratitude of this Seleucus does
     Even make me wild – O slave, of no more trust
     Than love that's hired! What, goest thou back? Thou
       shalt
     Go back, I warrant thee; but I'll catch thine eyes,
     Though they had wings. Slave, soulless villain, dog!
     O rarely base!

CAESAR   Good queen, let us entreat you.

CLEOPATRA

160   O Caesar, what a wounding shame is this,
     That thou vouchsafing here to visit me,

---

139 *brief* catalogue   146 *seel* sew up   152 *Mine* i.e., my followers   153 *estates* positions

Doing the honor of thy lordliness
To one so meek, that mine own servant should
Parcel the sum of my disgraces by   164
Addition of his envy. Say, good Caesar,
That I some lady trifles have reserved,   166
Immoment toys, things of such dignity   167
As we greet modern friends withal; and say   168
Some nobler token I have kept apart
For Livia and Octavia, to induce   170
Their mediation – must I be unfolded
With one that I have bred? The gods! It smites me 172
Beneath the fall I have. *[To Seleucus]* Prithee go hence,
Or I shall show the cinders of my spirits   174
Through th' ashes of my chance. Wert thou a man, 175
Thou wouldst have mercy on me.
CAESAR   Forbear, Seleucus.
                        [Exit Seleucus.]

CLEOPATRA
Be it known that we, the greatest, are misthought 177
For things that others do; and, when we fall,
We answer others' merits in our name,   179
Are therefore to be pitied.   *180*
CAESAR   Cleopatra,
Not what you have reserved nor what acknowledged
Put we i' th' roll of conquest. Still be't yours,
Bestow it at your pleasure, and believe   183
Caesar's no merchant, to make price with you   184
Of things that merchants sold. Therefore be cheered,
Make not your thoughts your prisons. No, dear queen, 186
For we intend so to dispose you as   187
Yourself shall give us counsel. Feed and sleep.

---

164 *Parcel* (1) number, (2) add to **166** *lady* feminine **167** *Immoment* insignificant **168** *modern* common **170** *Livia* Caesar's wife **172** *With* by **174** *cinders* embers **175** *chance* fortune **177** *misthought* misjudged **179** *merits . . . name* misdeeds done in our name (as if Seleucus had falsified the inventory for his own gain) **183** *Bestow* use **184** *make price* appraise **186** *Make . . . prisons* i.e., only in your own conceptions are you a prisoner **187** *you* of you

Our care and pity is so much upon you
190   That we remain your friend; and so adieu.

CLEOPATRA
My master, and my lord!

CEASAR   Not so. Adieu.
                    Flourish. Exeunt Caesar and his train.

CLEOPATRA
192   He words me, girls, he words me, that I should not
193   Be noble to myself. But hark thee, Charmian.
          [Whispers to Charmian.]

IRAS
Finish, good lady; the bright day is done,
And we are for the dark.

CLEOPATRA   Hie thee again.
I have spoke already, and it is provided;
Go put it to the haste.

CHARMIAN   Madam, I will.
      Enter Dolabella.

DOLABELLA
Where's the queen?

CHARMIAN   Behold, sir.   *[Exit.]*

CLEOPATRA   Dolabella!

DOLABELLA
Madam, as thereto sworn, by your command,
200   Which my love makes religion to obey,
I tell you this: Caesar through Syria
Intends his journey, and within three days
You with your children will he send before.
Make your best use of this. I have performed
Your pleasure and my promise.

CLEOPATRA   Dolabella,
I shall remain your debtor.

DOLABELLA   I, your servant.
Adieu, good queen; I must attend on Caesar.

CLEOPATRA
Farewell, and thanks.   *Exit [Dolabella].*

---

192 *words* deceives with words   **193** *noble* i.e., by suicide

                     Now, Iras, what think'st thou?
Thou, an Egyptian puppet, shall be shown
In Rome as well as I. Mechanic slaves   210
With greasy aprons, rules, and hammers shall
Uplift us to the view. In their thick breaths,
Rank of gross diet, shall we be enclouded,   213
And forced to drink their vapor.

IRAS   The gods forbid!

CLEOPATRA
Nay, 'tis most certain, Iras. Saucy lictors   215
Will catch at us like strumpets, and scald rhymers   216
Ballad us out o' tune. The quick comedians
Extemporally will stage us, and present
Our Alexandrian revels; Antony
Shall be brought drunken forth, and I shall see   220
Some squeaking Cleopatra boy my greatness   221
I' th' posture of a whore.

IRAS   O the good gods!

CLEOPATRA
Nay, that's certain.

IRAS
I'll never see't! For I am sure my nails
Are stronger than mine eyes.

CLEOPATRA   Why, that's the way
To fool their preparation, and to conquer
Their most absurd intents.
    Enter Charmian.   Now, Charmian!
Show me, my women, like a queen. Go fetch
My best attires. I am again for Cydnus,   229
To meet Mark Antony. Sirrah Iras, go.   230
Now, noble Charmian, we'll dispatch indeed,
And when thou hast done this chare, I'll give thee leave   232

---

210 *Mechanic slaves* i.e., manual laborers 213 *Rank of* offensive because of
215 *Saucy lictors* insolent officers 216 *scald* scabby 221 *squeaking* i.e., because women's parts were acted by adolescent boys; *boy* satirize 229–30
again . . . Antony (Enobarbus describes this meeting, II.2.200 ff.) 232 *chare*
chore

> To play till doomsday. – Bring our crown and all.
> > > > *[Exit Iras.] A noise within.*
> Wherefore's this noise?
> > *Enter a Guardsman.*

GUARD   Here is a rural fellow
> That will not be denied your highness' presence:
> He brings you figs.

CLEOPATRA
> Let him come in.   *Exit Guardsman.*
> > > What poor an instrument
> May do a noble deed! He brings me liberty.
239 My resolution's placed, and I have nothing
240 Of woman in me. Now from head to foot
> I am marble-constant; now the fleeting moon
242 No planet is of mine.
> > *Enter Guardsman and Clown [with basket].*

GUARD   This is the man.

CLEOPATRA
243 Avoid, and leave him.   *Exit Guardsman.*
244 Hast thou the pretty worm of Nilus there,
> That kills and pains not?

CLOWN   Truly I have him; but I would not be the party
> that should desire you to touch him, for his biting is
248 immortal: those that do die of it do seldom or never re-
> cover.

250 CLEOPATRA   Remember'st thou any that have died on't?

CLOWN   Very many, men and women too. I heard of one
252 of them no longer than yesterday; a very honest
253 woman, but something given to lie, as a woman should
> not do but in the way of honesty – how she died of the
> biting of it, what pain she felt. Truly, she makes a very
> good report o' th' worm; but he that will believe all that

---

239 *placed* fixed   242 s.d. *Clown* rural laborer   243 *Avoid* go   244 *worm*
serpent (asp)   248 *immortal* mortal – i.e., deadly (the Clown makes significant verbal substitutions and puns throughout his speeches)   250 *died* (also
slang for sexual climax)   252 *honest* (1) truth-telling, (2) sexually chaste
253 *lie* (1) tell falsehoods, (2) engage in sexual intercourse

they say shall never be saved by half that they do. But
this is most falliable, the worm's an odd worm.   258

CLEOPATRA   Get thee hence, farewell.

CLOWN   I wish you all joy of the worm.   260
[Sets down his basket.]

CLEOPATRA   Farewell.

CLOWN   You must think this, look you, that the worm
will do his kind.   263

CLEOPATRA   Ay, ay; farewell.

CLOWN   Look you, the worm is not to be trusted but in
the keeping of wise people, for indeed there is no goodness in the worm.

CLEOPATRA   Take thou no care, it shall be heeded.

CLOWN   Very good. Give it nothing, I pray you, for it is
not worth the feeding.   270

CLEOPATRA   Will it eat me?

CLOWN   You must not think I am so simple but I know
the devil himself will not eat a woman. I know that a
woman is a dish for the gods, if the devil dress her not.   274
But truly, these same whoreson devils do the gods great   275
harm in their women, for in every ten that they make,
the devils mar five.

CLEOPATRA   Well, get thee gone, farewell.

CLOWN   Yes, forsooth. I wish you joy o' th' worm.   *Exit.*
[Enter Iras with a robe, crown, etc.]

CLEOPATRA

Give me my robe, put on my crown; I have   280
Immortal longings in me. Now no more
The juice of Egypt's grape shall moist this lip.
Yare, yare, good Iras; quick. Methinks I hear   283
Antony call. I see him rouse himself
To praise my noble act. I hear him mock

---

258 *falliable* i.e., infallible   **263** *his kind* i.e., what may be expected from his
species   **274** *dress* (1) clothe, (2) prepare for eating   **275** *whoreson* (a common Elizabethan term of abuse, not meant literally here)   **280** (this episode
recalls Antony's dressing in IV.4)   **283** *Yare* nimbly

The luck of Caesar, which the gods give men
287   To excuse their after wrath. Husband, I come:
Now to that name my courage prove my title!
289   I am fire and air; my other elements
290   I give to baser life. So, have you done?
Come then, and take the last warmth of my lips.
Farewell, kind Charmian, Iras, long farewell.
          [Kisses them. Iras falls and dies.]
293   Have I the aspic in my lips? Dost fall?
If thou and nature can so gently part,
The stroke of death is as a lover's pinch,
Which hurts, and is desired. Dost thou lie still?
If thus thou vanishest, thou tell'st the world
It is not worth leave-taking.
CHARMIAN
Dissolve, thick cloud, and rain, that I may say
300   The gods themselves do weep.
CLEOPATRA   This proves me base:
301   If she first meet the curlèd Antony,
He'll make demand of her, and spend that kiss
Which is my heaven to have. Come, thou mortal
    wretch,
          [To an asp, which she applies to her breast]
304   With thy sharp teeth this knot intrinsicate
Of life at once untie. Poor venomous fool,
306   Be angry, and dispatch. O, couldst thou speak,
That I might hear thee call great Caesar ass
308   Unpolicied!
CHARMIAN   O eastern star!
CLEOPATRA   Peace, peace!
Dost thou not see my baby at my breast,
310   That sucks the nurse asleep?

---

287 *excuse . . . wrath* justify later ill fortune (or divine punishment) **289**
fire and air (the lighter of the four elements, thought of as belonging to im-
mortality); *other elements* i.e., water and earth, the heavier elements, be-
queathed by Cleopatra to mortality **293** *aspic* asp **301** *curlèd* curly-haired
304 *intrinsicate* entangled **306** *dispatch* make haste **308** *Unpolicied* out-
witted; *eastern star* the planet, hence the goddess, Venus

CHARMIAN   O, break! O, break!

CLEOPATRA

As sweet as balm, as soft as air, as gentle –

O Antony! Nay, I will take thee too:

[Applies another asp to her arm.]

What should I stay –

Dies.

CHARMIAN

In this wild world? So, fare thee well.

Now boast thee, death, in thy possession lies

A lass unparalleled. Downy windows, close;

And golden Phoebus never be beheld

Of eyes again so royal! Your crown's awry;

I'll mend it, and then play –

Enter the Guard, rustling in.

FIRST GUARD

Where's the queen?   320

CHARMIAN   Speak softly, wake her not.

FIRST GUARD

Caesar hath sent –

CHARMIAN   Too slow a messenger.

[To a third asp]

O, come apace, dispatch, I partly feel thee.

FIRST GUARD

Approach, ho! All's not well: Caesar's beguiled.   323

SECOND GUARD

There's Dolabella sent from Caesar. Call him.

FIRST GUARD

What work is here! Charmian, is this well done?

CHARMIAN

It is well done, and fitting for a princess

Descended of so many royal kings.

Ah, soldier!

Charmian dies.

Enter Dolabella.

———

323 *beguiled* tricked

DOLABELLA
  How goes it here?
SECOND GUARD   All dead.
DOLABELLA   Caesar, thy thoughts
330   Touch their effects in this. Thyself art coming
    To see performed the dreaded act which thou
    So sought'st to hinder.
        Enter Caesar and all his train, marching.
ALL   A way there, a way for Caesar!
DOLABELLA
  O sir, you are too sure an augurer;
  That you did fear is done.
CAESAR   Bravest at the last,
335   She leveled at our purposes and, being royal,
    Took her own way. The manner of their deaths?
    I do not see them bleed.
DOLABELLA   Who was last with them?
FIRST GUARD
  A simple countryman, that brought her figs.
  This was his basket.
CAESAR   Poisoned, then.
FIRST GUARD   O Caesar,
340   This Charmian lived but now; she stood and spake.
    I found her trimming up the diadem
    On her dead mistress; tremblingly she stood,
    And on the sudden dropped.
CAESAR   O noble weakness!
    If they had swallowed poison, 'twould appear
    By external swelling; but she looks like sleep,
    As she would catch another Antony
347   In her strong toil of grace.
DOLABELLA   Here on her breast
348   There is a vent of blood, and something blown;
    The like is on her arm.

---

330 *Touch their effects* meet fulfillment   **335** *leveled at* guessed   **347** *toil* net
348 *vent* discharge; *blown* swelled

FIRST GUARD

    This is an aspic's trail, and these fig leaves   *350*

    Have slime upon them, such as th' aspic leaves

    Upon the caves of Nile.

CAESAR   Most probable

    That so she died; for her physician tells me

    She hath pursued conclusions infinite   354

    Of easy ways to die. Take up her bed,   355

    And bear her women from the monument.

    She shall be buried by her Antony.

    No grave upon the earth shall clip in it   358

    A pair so famous. High events as these

    Strike those that make them; and their story is   360

    No less in pity than his glory which

    Brought them to be lamented. Our army shall

    In solemn show attend this funeral,

    And then to Rome. Come, Dolabella, see

    High order in this great solemnity.   *Exeunt.*

---

354 *conclusions* experiments   355 *die* (one last sexual pun: see I.2.138 n.)
358 *clip* clasp   360 *Strike* touch

The distinguished Pelican Shakespeare series, newly revised to be the premier choice for students, professors, and general readers well into the 21st century

NOW AVAILABLE

Antony and Cleopatra
ISBN 0-14-071452-9

The Comedy of Errors
ISBN 0-14-071474-X

Coriolanus
ISBN 0-14-071473-1

Cymbeline
ISBN 0-14-071472-3

Henry IV, Part I
ISBN 0-14-071456-1

Henry IV, Part 2
ISBN 0-14-071457-X

Henry V
ISBN 0-14-071458-8

King Lear
ISBN 0-14-071476-6

King Lear (The Quarto and Folio Texts)
ISBN 0-14-071490-1

Macbeth
ISBN 0-14-071478-2

Much Ado About Nothing
ISBN 0-14-071480-4

The Narrative Poems
ISBN 0-14-071481-2

Richard III
ISBN 0-14-071483-9

Romeo and Juliet
ISBN 0-14-071484-7

The Tempest
ISBN 0-14-071485-5

Timon of Athens
ISBN 0-14-071487-1

Titus Andronicus
ISBN 0-14-071491-X

Twelfth Night
ISBN 0-14-071489-8

The Two Gentlemen of Verona
ISBN 0-14-071461-8

The Winter's Tale
ISBN 0-14-071488-X

FORTHCOMING

All's Well That Ends Well
ISBN 0-14-071460-X

As You Like It
ISBN 0-14-071471-5

Hamlet
ISBN 0-14-071454-5

Henry VI, Part 1
ISBN 0-14-071465-0

Henry VI, Part 2
ISBN 0-14-071466-9

Henry VI, Part 3
ISBN 0-14-071467-7

Henry VIII
ISBN 0-14-071475-8

Julius Caesar
ISBN 0-14-071468-5

King John
ISBN 0-14-071459-6

Love's Labor's Lost
ISBN 0-14-071477-4

Measure for Measure
ISBN 0-14-071479-0

The Merchant of Venice
ISBN 0-14-071462-6

The Merry Wives of Windsor
ISBN 0-14-071464-2

A Midsummer Night's Dream
ISBN 0-14-071455-3

Othello
ISBN 0-14-071463-4

Pericles
ISBN 0-14-071469-3

Richard II
ISBN 0-14-071482-0

The Sonnets
ISBN 0-14-071453-7

The Taming of the Shrew
ISBN 0-14-071451-0

Troilus and Cressida
ISBN 0-14-071486-3